MINISTERING TO
ABORTION'S
AFTERMATH

Bill and Sue Banks

GOOD NEWS CRUSADE
(BOOKSHOP)
15/17, HIGH CROSS STREET
ST. AUSTELL, CORNWALL
ENGLAND PL25 4AN
TELEPHONE: 0726 63945

Preface

The purpose of this book is not primarily to persuade women to avoid having abortions, although it is our prayer that this will indeed be a by-product of presenting this material. Our goal is rather to assist those who have already had an abortion and those seeking to minister aid to them. We hope to help these women to understand themselves and to deal with their feelings of guilt, self-condemnation and depression. Most of all we desire to point the way to the only true and effective source of help . . . Jesus Christ!

Abortion has reached epidemic proportions in this country. Since the legalization of abortion in the United States in 1973, the slaughter of more than ten million unborn babies in "legal" operations has been recorded. The inhumane death record of Hitler's concentration camps has already been surpassed in our "moral," "Christian" country. It is estimated that more than 60% of these abortions have been performed upon unmarried women, and that less than 5% have had *any* medical justification.

These are staggering statistics, and there is a word which covers each of these factors . . . Sin!

If you are one of those who has had an abortion and have been tormented with feelings of guilt, shame, lack of self-worth, fear of being found out, self-hate, unhappiness, depression and perhaps even thoughts of suicide, let me assure you that there is HOPE! Jesus has provided deliverance for all those who are willing to repent, cease from their own efforts of rationalization and self-justification, and who come to Him, humbly without excuse, throwing themselves upon His mercy.

Jesus not only *can*, but He *desires* to set you free. What

He has done for the women whose stories are related in this book, He can do for you!

Dedication

It is with profound gratitude and respect that we dedicate this book to those who have "pioneered" in the field of deliverance, who have born the shame, the reproach, and have continued to hold forth the lamp of God's truth; *to pioneers* such as Maxwell Whyte, Derek Prince and men of like calibre who have enlightened, edified and equipped the Body. . . . And *to the "Finger of God"* — the power of the Holy Spirit which has enabled Jesus and His followers to cast out demons . . . and *to you* whom the Lord desires to use to break Satan's chains of bondage.

Our prayer is that this book will in some way contribute to "setting the captives free"!

The following accounts are related in order that you might have your hopes lifted, and your faith built to seek Him whose very name[1] means total deliverance.

> "And it shall come to pass, that whosoever shall call on the name of the Lord shall be delivered . . ." (Joel 2:32).

> ". . . And call upon me in the day of trouble: I will deliver thee and thou shalt glorify me" (Psalm 50:15).

[1] Jesus = Yeshua = Salvation: Total salvation encompassing every facet of your personality and life (body, soul, spirit) and from every type of danger — be it physical, financial, emotional, mental or from enemies, total deliverance!

Foreword

Christian counsellors and deliverance ministers deal regularly with the consequences of sin in people's lives. Many have committed sins of ignorance, not realizing that what they have done is sinful. So it has been with abortion. In the world the debate continues as to the right or wrong of abortion, but in the Kingdom of God the question is settled — abortion is the sin of murder.

Even if one has agreed with abortion he has committed murder already in his heart. Not only the woman who has had an abortion needs forgiveness for the sin of murder, but also each person who has counselled, assisted or agreed with that abortion. This is in accord with the teaching of Jesus in Matthew 5:21, 22, 27, 28.

The truth that abortion is murder must be shouted from the housetops. The Bible warns of impending judgement upon a nation when the people "call evil good and good evil" (Isaiah 5:20). God says children are "the heritage of the Lord" (Psalm 127:3), and He blesses the righteous with fruitfulness in childbearing (Deuteronomy 28:4).

Those who promote abortion are calling child-bearing evil and murder good. But God's grace provides forgiveness and deliverance for all who repent and call upon Him.

We pray the Lord will bless this book on abortion. It is such a needed thing.

— Frank D. Hammond

Table of Contents

PART ONE

Abortion Is Seen to Be Murder

My own firsthand experience with the problem of abortion began early in 1972 when I encountered a woman troubled with what turned out to be a case of *abortion's aftermath!*

Abortion Is Murder!

CASE NO. 1: EDNA

"Yea, they sacrificed their sons and their daughters unto devils, and *shed innocent blood,* even the blood of their sons and of their daughters, whom they sacrificed unto the idols of Canaan: and the land was polluted with blood" (Psalm 106:37, 38).

"But your *iniquities have separated* between you and your God, and your sins have hid his face from you, that he will not hear. For your hands are defiled with blood, and your fingers with iniquity; your lips have spoken lies, your tongue hath muttered perverseness" (Isaiah 59:2-3).

". . . Because of the wickedness of thy doings, . . . thy heaven that is over thy head shall be brass . . ." (Deuteronomy 28:20, 23).

Edna's Story

Edna[2], an early leader in the Charismatic movement in St. Louis, came to visit me one afternoon and said, "I really don't

[2]The names throughout this book have been changed for obvious reasons (except for Case No. 12). The cases are otherwise factual.

3

know what's wrong with me, or even why I wanted to see you, but I feel somehow as if I just can't make any progress with God lately. I seem to be at a standstill. I'm still praying, praying in the Spirit, and reading my Bible regularly, but it doesn't seem to help. I feel as if I'm only going through the motions. I sense something down deep inside which causes me to feel separated from God, and I feel as if my prayers aren't being heard (even though I know intellectually that they are). I just can't seem to get any victory."

"Have you any areas of unconfessed sin that might be causing you guilt, or blocking your relationship with God?" I asked her rather bluntly.

"No, I've thought of that and I've searched myself. I can't think of anything at all," she replied thoughtfully. Hesitatingly she added, "Well, there is one thing, but I've already confessed it and it's 'under the blood.' "

"What's that one thing, Edna?" I inquired.

"I had an abortion about twenty years ago before I was married. But, of course, that's so long ago, and besides since becoming a Christian several years ago, I have confessed it to the Lord and asked His forgiveness for the sin involved and for the abortion. . . ." By the time she had finished that sentence, tears had begun to flow. "I guess maybe I'm not quite as free, after all, as I thought that I was." She continued trying to smile.

"Have you confessed the sin of abortion as also being the sin of *murder?*" I asked. "Because that is how God views it. It is *murder* in His sight."

"No, I haven't." She began to sob heavily, "But I will."

Seeing her readiness and the obvious conviction of her heart, I lead her in a prayer confessing the abortion itself as a sin, as well as the sin which led to the need for the abortion, and then also confessing it as the sin of *murder.*

4

We then in agreement commanded the *spirits*[3] *of abortion* and *murder* to come out of her. She let out a broken-hearted wail (in which I felt I could hear the cry of grief of a mother who had just lost a child) sobbed a few times more, and then peace evidently began flooding into her, as she relaxed and began to smile broadly.

"Wow!" she said wiping away the remaining tears with a tissue. "I would never have believed that *I* had an evil spirit nor that abortion could have caused all that; but, bless God, now I'm free!"

Nearly ten years have elapsed and this woman is still a joy-infused member of the local body of Christ, ministering in our area.

Observations

1. This was the first time we had ever come against the *spirit of abortion* but we had heard anointed teaching previously which had prepared us to be able to help her. Simply knowing the truth, *that abortion is viewed by God as murder*, and having the boldness to present that fact to her brought deliverance. This truth literally set her free.

2. She didn't believe that a Christian could have a demon (or "be demonized" to be more accurate) until she herself was set free. This has been the experience of many.

3. Having the evil spirit didn't prevent her from being a Spirit-baptized Christian, but it served to curtail her joy and to sap her spiritual strength, robbing her of energy that would have enabled her to serve the Lord more effectively.

4. Confession of the abortion merely as abortion hadn't brought freedom, nor broken the evil spirit's hold.

[3]If you are a minister, counsellor, or a victim and do not believe in the existence of demons, don't let that prevent you from reading on. Simply put the issue of the reality of demons on a "back burner" and let the Lord either confirm or disprove the matter for you. Please don't "throw the baby out with the bath." Take abortion seriously and pray about it; pray with the people whom you counsel about it — their lives literally may depend upon you doing so!

5. The fact that the sin had occurred many years in the past had not eliminated either the guilt, nor freed her from the harassment of the evil spirit. The passage of time has no bearing as the next case will also serve to illustrate.

Indicators (of a need for ministry)

OUTWARDLY OBSERVABLE SYMPTOMS (offering clues to the one ministering)

1. None

INWARD SYMPTOMS (offering clues to the candidate)

1. Apparently none for years

2. At point of seeking ministry:
   a. A feeling of growth in God being blocked
   b. A feeling of separation from God

Abortion
Is Premeditated Murder

CASE NO. 2: NANCY

"Thou shalt not kill" (Exodus 20:13).

"There shall not be found among you any one that maketh his son or his daughter to pass through the fire (i.e. infant sacrifice). . . . For all that do these things are an abomination unto the Lord . . ." (Deuteronomy 18:10, 12).

Nancy's Story

Another of the early cases which we encountered requiring deliverance from a *spirit of abortion* or actually *murder*, was that of a lady named Nancy who came to us from the West Coast. Nancy thought, as we did, that she was coming to our prayer room to receive the Baptism in the Holy Spirit, but the Lord, it seems, had more in store for her.

After a preliminary conversation, she in a rather matter-of-fact manner said, "Well, I *do want to* receive the Baptism in the Holy Spirit, but I don't think that I can."

Somewhat taken aback, I asked her, "Why on earth do you think that you cannot receive the Baptism?"

She replied rather reluctantly, "Well, I have committed a sin."

I smiled as I told her, "That's not uncommon, and fortunately it doesn't make one ineligible for God's blessings. All of us have sinned in the past and fallen short of the glory which God intended for us. If having sinned would make one ineligible, how could anyone ever hope to receive? Besides if we were already sinlessly perfect, we probably wouldn't need the Baptism anyway. Have you confessed your sin to the Lord?" I asked.

She quickly responded, "Oh yes. I've confessed it many, many times."

"But, you obviously don't feel free from it then?" I asked, and she nodded sorrowfully. I didn't like what she had said from a theological standpoint, for I felt that if she had indeed, validly repented of the sin and confessed it, she should have been freed from the guilt of the sin. Somewhat perplexed, I continued, "What then was your sin?"

Nancy confessed remorsefully, "I had an abortion, but," she quickly added, "it was over thirty years ago that I had it. I have been in and out of mental institutions ever since. For more than thirty years, I have been tormented and sought help, but the mental institutions and all the doctors and all the psychiatrists haven't been able to help me."

Her plight reminded me of the account in the Scriptures of the woman who had been "nothing bettered, but rather grew worse" after spending all her living seeking medical help (Mark 5:25, 26).

7

The medical professions had been unable to help Nancy, at least unable to free her of her guilt or to restore her fully to a normal life. I then asked her bluntly, "Have you confessed this to the Lord as the sin of abortion?" When she responded in the affirmative, I continued, "Have you also confessed it to the Lord as the sin of murder? If not, you need to because that is how God views it!"

Nancy immediately began to cry and sobbed out broken heartedly, *"I've known it was murder from before the time I committed it!"*

I then suggested that she confess right then to the Lord, with me serving as her witness, that she had committed the sin of abortion and had also committed the sin of murder, which she did. After Nancy had repented of the sin and confessed it to the Lord as murder, I then took authority over the *spirits of murder* and *abortion* which had been tormenting her for so many years, and cast them out in Jesus' name.

Nancy trembled, cried and shook violently; coughed as someone might who had a bit of food lodged in the throat, and then heaved a great sigh of relief signalling victory was attained. A smile began spreading over her face for the first time since I had met her. Nancy then received the Baptism in the Holy Spirit and began rejoicing in a new prayer language![4] She walked out of the prayer room, visibly a different person: truly a new creation. The worn, drawn, haggard expression which had been upon her face when she arrived, Jesus had removed and replaced with an expression of radiant joy.

As an interesting sidelight, whenever Nancy passes through our city, she drops in to see me to say hello, and to thank me for praying with her. She is today as radiant a joy-filled Christian as she was that day when she walked out of our prayer room over eight years ago.

This was one of the earliest cases where God allowed us to see, literally, the visible, tangible effect of someone being

---

[4]For a more complete and detailed explanation of the Baptism in the Holy Spirit and "praying in tongues" we recommend the book *Alive Again!* by the same author.

ministered to, and being set free from the *spirits* of *abortion* and *murder*.

Observations

1. The enemy had been able to do a work of unbelief upon Nancy convincing her that she was unworthy and unable to receive from the Lord something which she greatly desired.

2. Confessing abortion as abortion, even many times, wasn't sufficient to break Satan's hold upon her. Not until the true nature of the sin was both recognized and confessed as being murder did she obtain freedom.

3. Satan's primary area of attack upon Nancy was in the mental realm. Sometimes he also attacks physically but most commonly it seems to be chiefly in the area of robbing the woman of peace and joy, and actually tormenting her with guilt and fears. Note: The woman often may not associate these mental problems with her having had the abortion, especially since many of those counselling such patients will tell them that what they've done is neither legally nor *morally* wrong, thus serving further to block their path to the real source of help: confession to and cleansing from Jesus.

4. She *knew* that the abortion was *murder* from *before* the time that she actually obtained it. Rarely, if ever, is the woman truly unaware of the sin aspect of the abortion, although she may push all thought of guilt related to the sin from her conscious mind. God has written this truth in the heart of the woman. This is the reason why the consciences of women convict them; they are being convicted upon the basis of God's word and God's law — not upon that of man's opinion or views. The *CONSCIENCE CONVICTS UPON THE BASIS OF GOD'S WORD AND GOD'S LAWS*. No amount of counselling can ever set someone completely free from the guilt of sin without

9

recourse to the forgiveness and the shed blood of Jesus Christ.

5. Joy entered this woman's life probably for the first time and her physical appearance actually changed. She appeared to be considerably younger because of the weight of sin which Jesus had lifted from her shoulders.

6. My bluntness, incidentally, in calling a "spade a spade," was really a kindness, because I was presenting Jesus' truth to her. Just as a splinter must be removed, in spite of the momentary pain, to permit complete healing to occur, so, too, truth, even painful truth, must be stated in order to set someone free.

Indicators (of a need for ministry)

OUTWARDLY OBSERVABLE SYMPTOMS (offering clues to the one ministering)

1. Apparent mental illness . . . unresolvable by medical means

2. Lack of joy

INWARD SYMPTOMS (offering clues to the candidate)

1. Guilt

2. Torment

3. Fear, pressure

The world wants us to believe that life doesn't commence until a baby is born, but what is the real truth? God's word gave us the answer.

TEACHING SECTION I

Abortion is the law of the land. Why do you object to it?
Why do you state that abortion is murder?
When does life begin? Have you any proof?

I. The fetus is a person!

   A. Some logical medical considerations

   B. Life begins at conception

SOME LOGICAL MEDICAL CONSIDERATIONS

Performing abortions is dangerous in the natural realm and very dangerous from the point of view of Scripture. It is also not in line with the ethics of the medical profession.

"Cursed be he that taketh reward to slay the innocent person" (Deuteronomy 27:25).

"Whoso sheddeth man's blood, by man shall his blood be shed" (Genesis 9:6).

Today the medical profession still takes the Hippocratic Oath which contains the following: "To none will I give a deadly drug, even if solicited, nor offer counsel to such an end, and no woman will I give a destructive suppository, but guiltless and hallowed will I keep my art."

Abortion has been offered as a panacea for women. Rather than solving problems for women it has been shown to cause deep-seated guilt, depression, and often mental illness. Conversely the pro-abortionists tell us that the mental health of the mother will be adversely affected by having an unwanted child. However, studies on suicide have shown that neither pregnant women nor those with illegitimate pregnancies are any more prone to take their lives than are other categories of individuals.

The same group would also have us believe that the fetus isn't a person and thus can have no rights of its own . . . because for the first 24 weeks of its life it could not survive on its own without the life supports and protection offered by its mother's body. If we pursue this same rationale, most unconscious patients, accident victims and many in hospitals who couldn't survive without outside life-supporting plasma, glucose, and the protection or care offered by the nurses and hospital staff could have their lives terminated upon the decision of their relatives or physicians. The victim or patient is every bit as dependent as the fetus whose destruction is rationalized for the reason of being unable to survive on its own.

Several physicians have gone on record that abortion is

never necessary to save the life of the mother. This is quite contrary to the standard rhetoric offered by the pro-abortionist forces. They would have us to believe that abortion is safer than carrying a baby full term and going through normal delivery. This is patently false. Normal childbirth is not usually dangerous to the life of the mother. Abortion, on the other hand, is not natural and is normally quite a bit more dangerous and definitely requires more care and medical precaution than does normal childbirth. In October of 1981 a mentally retarded inmate at a state institution located in Saint Louis, Missouri, was sent to a hospital to have an abortion performed, and *died as a result of the procedure.* It is not a simple, totally safe operation as we have been led to believe.

A Heavenly Thought

When we reach heaven, we will meet there the spirits of those who die before birth, as well as those who die later in life. This truth is of special comfort to those who have lost children through miscarriage or at birth. I recall one lovely young woman asking me if her two children whom she had lost through miscarriage had spirits and if she would get to see them in heaven.

I didn't have a well thought out answer, but the Holy Spirit quickened truth to me on the spot. I told her that on the basis of John the Baptist being filled with the Holy Spirit while yet in his mother's womb, obviously the fetus had both spiritual capacity and personality. I then told her I was certain that she would eventually see her two still-born sons in heaven.

Children are, and always have been, considered to be a *blessing* in almost all cultures, and are especially considered to be such in Scripture.

Jesus said in Luke 18:16, "Suffer little children to come unto me . . . for of such is the kingdom of God."

Sarah was blessed:

13

"And I will *bless her*, and give thee a son also of her" (Genesis 17:16).

Rebekah was blessed:

Isaac prayed for his barren wife and in answer to his prayer: "the Lord was entreated of him, and Rebekah his wife conceived" (Genesis 25:21).

Hannah was blessed:

Hannah pleaded with God and received an answer: "For this child I prayed; and the Lord hath given me my petition" (I Samuel 1:27).

Children are a blessing and in these examples and thousands of other cases, the children came as answers to prayers.

When does life begin? How can you know?

LIFE BEGINS AT CONCEPTION:
A fetus is *a living soul — a person* from conception:

"Behold, *I* was shapen in iniquity; and in sin did *my* mother conceive *me*" (Psalm 51:5).

"thou. . . hast covered *me* in *my mother's womb* . . . *I* was made in secret . . . *my* substance, yet being unperfect . . . *my* members were written . . . when as yet there was none of them . . ." (Psalm 139:13-16).

". . . The Lord hath *called me* from *the womb*; from the bowels of *my* mother hath he made mention of *my* name" (Isaiah 49:1).

"Before I formed thee in the belly I *knew thee*; and before *thou* camest forth out of the womb I *sanctified thee*, and I *ordained thee a prophet* unto the nations" (Jeremiah 1:5).

In each of these four representative passages we see the Lord taking action upon a person, a being, still in the womb of his mother.

This same view of pre-natal personhood, existing before

14

birth, is clearly evident in the New Testament also as exemplified by the case of John the Baptist. John, at age "conception-plus-six-months," *leaped for joy*. The person John reacted physically to a pleasant stimulus, and is recorded as having expressed an emotion — joy. Also we can note that his reaction was caused by the presence of the Son of God . . . who was still in the *womb* of *His mother*, Mary. Stated slightly differently, the *fetus* of John the Baptist rejoiced in reaction to the *fetus* of Jesus Christ.

Note: We have here: the *person* of John at age *birth-minus-three-months* reacting to the presence *of the person* of Jesus at age *birth-minus-six-months*. Both of them individual *persons* at six and three months post-conception (and pre-birth). It is also significant that Jesus took upon Himself *humanity!* When did He take humanity upon Himself?

I submit to you that He took humanity upon Himself the very instant when He allowed Himself to be implanted within the womb of Mary, by the Holy Spirit. He obviously had already done it by the time of the incident mentioned above. It is certain that He took upon Himself humanity when He voluntarily subjected Himself to the natural laws of this planet. Gravity for example had no effect upon Him one second prior to conception, but it obviously did afterwards.

Thus it seems clear from Scripture that when a child is conceived, it becomes a living soul! Scripturally speaking, "soul" means "life." When a fetus becomes alive (as it does at conception), it is a *soul:* it is a *person*. This same premise, interestingly enough, is observed by the laws of our land. Rather than treating a fetus to be a non-entity as the recent abortion law would like to have it viewed, the courts of our land have maintained that the unborn child from the point of conception is a person for purposes of tort law. The effect of this is that the unborn child has certain rights, and to cause its death as by an attack upon the mother is a crime punishable by law. The loss of the child is usually considered a loss of value to the parents and they are able to seek compensation for the death and loss of their unborn child. Abortion is viewed as a crime in virtually all civilized countries of the world.

The gradual acceptance of abortion has paralleled the acceptance of other behavior destructive to the human family and human personality such as adultery, divorce, and homosexuality. Where abortion is prevalent, so also is an overall hardening of the consciences of the people of that nation.

Recent developments in the medical field have made it possible to perform inter-uteran surgical procedures upon the occupant of the womb. This is further evidence that the fetus is a person. Such procedures recognize that the fetus is a person, is alive, is a savable or treatable life. The doctors so operating are clearly stating by their actions that the occupant of the womb is an important individual, worth treating, worth their efforts and is a valuable part of society. At the very least they are stating that the fetus is an object of their responsibility and has a right to life.

Little did we suspect, in spite of the medical logic supporting the truths which the Lord had revealed unto us, that our next contact would be with a medical doctor whom the Lord would use to teach us more about Satan's involvement with abortion.

PART TWO

Abortion Reveals
Satan's Hatred for Children

.

Abortion May Reflect or Manifest as . . .
Hatred of Children

CASE NO. 3: DR. LUKE

"The tender and delicate woman . . . her *eye shall be evil toward the husband* of her bosom, and toward her son, and toward her daughter, and *toward her young one that cometh out from between her feet,* and *toward her children* which she shall bear" (Deuteronomy 28:56, 57).

"Whosoever hateth his brother is a murderer: and ye know that no murderer hath eternal life abiding in him" (I John 3:15).

Dr. Luke's Story

As I sat across the table from Dr. Luke in the restaurant, I found myself wondering why we were having this meeting. He had called me the day before asking if I would have breakfast with him. He had only said that he wanted to meet me for breakfast so that we might be able to discuss some "spiritual matters." I was wondering why the Spirit had caused me to accept so vague an invitation, as I knew that normally I would not have without knowing more. As I studied his countenance there was no clue. He was a sweet-faced, almost cherubic looking, bubbly individual yet there was still something. . . .

The conversation interrupted my thoughts and continued

in a fairly light manner as we shared about the goodness and blessings of the Lord which we had both observed. His face suddenly became serious as he asked, "Do you believe in evil spirits, or demons? Is it possible for evil spirits to exist today; and especially is it possible for a Christian to have an evil spirit?" He paused thoughtfully and then continued, "I've heard much teaching that it is impossible for this to be, but I have questions." Dr. Luke then went on to state several of the common arguments as to why that couldn't be the case.

I explained my understanding of evil spirits briefly to him: that they existed when Jesus walked the streets in the flesh: the world is certainly no better today than it was then; if Jesus was correct in His assessment of the situation then, it is only logical to assume that they still exist today. I mentioned several experiences we had had with Christians and even Spirit Baptized Christians who had both needed and received deliverance from evil spirits. After citing several other examples, and some of the truths shared in Part One of this book, I then "happened" to choose as an illustration the subject of abortion as a means of exemplifying the truth we were discussing and gave the example of Nancy mentioned previously.

The color momentarily drained from his face and then came rushing back, his eyes lighting and he said, "Now I know why God has brought us together." Tears brimmed his eyes as he said, "*My wife* had an *abortion* years ago: and I think that is the key to all our problems."

"But Dr. Luke," I injected, "how could you as a Christian and especially as a doctor, sworn to save life, allow an abortion to be performed on your own child?"

He shook his head sadly, "I couldn't and *wouldn't* today, but back then I was in medical school and we both felt we couldn't afford a child at that time; nor would our careers permit the time it would cost. I know it sounds terribly selfish, but that was some of the pressure. I really didn't want the abortion, but my wife insisted, and her family wanted her to complete her education, so they sided with her. I would have been out-voted anyway if it had come down to that." He choked up, cleared his throat, and continued, "I cannot possibly put into words to try to describe to you, brother, what I felt in that hospital . . . what terrible emotions I experienced as I looked down into that surgical pan, and saw my "first-born" son lying there. I just can't tell you. . . ." He buried his face in his napkin.

Dr. Luke recovered himself and then continued, "I could never understand why my wife could, on the one hand, be a fine functioning Christian — happy, joyful and normal — and then as suddenly as turning the page of a book, she would reveal a side of her nature that seemed totally out of character, and she would manifest . . . *hatred* toward our kids." Tears again filled his eyes, and I could tell that it was extremely painful to him to even speak of these fears and problems which had been hidden in darkness for so long.

"That look . . ." he shuddered and went on, "that look on her face, as she would sometimes turn and lash out with such hatred toward the kids and even toward me! She unleashed such anger, such vehemence, such hatred and such violence as she would scream at them — I could almost believe that she wanted to *murder* them. I simply cannot understand what could possibly have brought this about (until your statement about *abortion being an evil spirit*).

He heaved a huge sigh as if glad to be finally able to speak of these things and to have them out in the light of day. As I waited silently for him to resume his story, he mentioned another symptom of her behavior which fit right into the developing pattern, "She hates anything to do with the Holy Spirit! She functions normally in a church situation as a Christian and I know she has been validly saved and water-baptized." He repeated himself thoughtfully, "She's validly saved, baptized in water . . . but she just hates anything to do with the Holy Spirit. In fact," he continued painfully, "she has delivered an ultimatum to me, and has said that if I so much as mention the Baptism in the Holy Spirit or even the Holy Spirit Himself to her again, that she will divorce me!"

This apparent facade of hers, one moment seeming completely normal and then allowing such hatred to manifest itself particularly toward the children, perplexed him, as it seemed to be so totally out of character with the rest of her personality and life.

Observations

1. "My people are destroyed for lack of knowledge" (Hosea 4:6). This doctor needed some truth, which he had not heard, and had not been taught, in order to confirm what God had already been impressing upon his heart. His questions about demons indicated to me that the Spirit had already been suggesting to him that his wife might need deliverance.

2. This woman was trying to function as a Christian — she was at least going through the motions — and was attending church. However, there was a demonic side of her nature which she was apparently unable to control, which would manifest at times un-Christlike emotions such as hatred.

3. She manifested hatred toward anything to do with the Holy Spirit — obviously an unnatural position for a Christian to take. I suspect that she may have had an unfortunate experience while herself seeking the Baptism in the Holy Spirit and not receiving it: being left feeling as if she were somehow discriminated against by the Lord. Unhappily this is not an uncommon experience where ministry is slip-shod, motivated more by zeal than the Spirit, and where sufficient time and love isn't devoted to the candidate for the Baptism.

4. Another possible explanation for her reaction toward the Holy Spirit could have been the natural hatred of the demons within her, motivating her response. People who need deliverance often fear both deliverance and the Holy Spirit. The fear of deliverance is readily understandable.

The fear of the Holy Spirit by these people is equally understandable when we consider that He is the instrument or power utilized by Jesus to cast out demons. (". . . I cast out devils by the Spirit of God . . ." Matthew 12:28).

5. Regardless of the exact cause of her attitude toward the Holy Spirit, the result was a heart hardened against God, His Spirit, and anyone truly attempting to serve Him. When ministry was offered her, she refused to admit the abortion as sin. She manifested both an unteachable nature and was uncooperative, and unwilling to receive ministry from the Lord. So far as I know this particular woman remains in her nest of hatred and unconfessed sin to this day. Please pray for her, and especially for her husband and children — and all like them in similar bondage or torments from Satan.

6. When one *refuses* to face or to deal with one area of sin (or one evil spirit) the contagion seems to spread and soon that sin (or spirit) is joined by others.

    NOTE: Having a demon is no disgrace: However *keeping one, once you are aware that you have it, is a problem.* God, of course, only holds us responsible for the truth or light that we possess. Satan on the other hand, will use any and all of our ignorance against us. He is no gentleman, and he doesn't fight fairly!

7. One demon, as we said, often leads to another. . . . The woman was threatening her husband with *divorce.* She was attempting to manipulate, to control, to dominate him — all of which are characteristics of *witchcraft.* Satan's intent was to prevent Dr. Luke from serving God up to his potential, which was great, and to keep him from causing *her* to turn from her sin, and to serve God.

8. A key point is also to be seen here in our failure to be able to minister to Dr. Luke's wife. She was *unwilling to confess her abortion as sin!* So long as she would not see it as

sin, she was of course, totally blocked from being able to receive forgiveness for it. The hardness of her heart was the block!

It seems almost too simple to bother stating, but, A PERSON MUST BE WILLING TO ADMIT THE SINFULNESS OF AN ACTION, IN ORDER TO BE ABLE TO CONFESS IT AND BE FORGIVEN FOR IT BY JESUS. So long as one tries to rationalize it, or justify it, that person is effectively blocked from taking it to Jesus.

9. The Holy Spirit had given Dr. Luke some additional insight, as evidenced by his comment that he somehow felt that *the key* to *all* their troubles was rooted in her having had the abortion.

10. It is interesting to note in this case, as we will see underscored in case No. 9, that those who have demonic problems in their lives often seem to wear masks so as not to have their problems detected by others. They will often go to great lengths to try to appear religious or pious or good.

Indicators (of a need for ministry)

OUTWARDLY OBSERVABLE SYMPTOMS (offering clues to the one ministering)

1. Wife showed behavior eccentricites; unstable relations with the children and family; outbursts of irrational anger toward children particularly.

2. Hatred of children manifested

3. Rejection of those who would offer spiritual help or prayer

INWARD SYMPTOMS (offering clues to the candidate)

1. None available

2. Probable torment and self hate

3. Heart apparently hardened which she may have realized

As Dr. Luke related his story, I couldn't help thinking back to the first deliverance ministry which had occurred after I read the manuscript for the book which we later published under the title, *Pigs in the Parlor.* I received the manuscript in the mail on a Friday, and had an immediate witness within my spirit that it was important and anointed. I took the manuscript home over the weekend and read it. When I returned to my office on the following Monday, the Lord brought into our adjoining bookstore, Alice, a woman who was obviously distraught, and as it turned out was to be a test case for some new truth which we had gleaned from *Pigs in the Parlor.*

Abortion Is Unnatural:
Leads to Condemnation and Can Lead to Suicide

CASE NO. 4: ALICE

"For no man ever yet *hateth his own flesh*" (Ephesians 5:29.

"In the last days . . . men shall be lovers of their own selves, covetous, boasters, proud, blasphemers, disobedient to parents, unthankful, unholy, *without natural affection* . . . lovers of pleasures more than lovers of God" (II Timothy 3:1-4).

Alice's Story

As I first began to speak with her, Alice burst into tears and then apologized for being so upset. I asked if she would care to step back into our prayer room for prayer. She nodded and I led her back to the prayer room. There over a cup of coffee, she began to pour out her troubles. She said, "I feel that I am a horrible person, an unnatural woman and am unfit to be called a Christian, even though I am a life-long Episcopalian. I have an unnatural characteristic. I hate to even mention it, but you see, I really am terrible . . . *I hate my own children!*"

As if for emphasis, she again repeated it, *"I hate my own children!* You see, I am really a terrible person! It will be difficult for you to believe or understand this, but it is physically repulsive — it is offensive for me to *touch my own children*, or even to *have them touch me.* You see, I CANNOT BE A NORMAL WOMAN. I couldn't really be a Christian and have feelings like this. It's definitely unnatural. I must really be a horrible, horrible person that God cannot spare me from this, or that I have to be this way!"

I then explained briefly to Alice about the demonic realm and how demons lust to manifest their natures through human bodies since they have no bodies of their own. I asked if she'd like to have me pray for her against demons, just in case they might be the source of her problems. I led her in a prayer and then commanded the spirit or spirits causing this unnatural reaction within her toward her own offspring to manifest itself and to come out. Five spirits eventually named themselves and came out of her that morning.

First was a spirit of *self-condemnation* or *self-hatred;* the second was the *spirit of abortion and murder;* the third was a spirit which caused her to *hate her own children;* and fourth was *repulsion to the touch of her own children.* When that spirit named itself and came out, she fell to her knees out of the chair where she had been sitting, laughing and crying all at the same time and praising God. The words tumbling forth from her lips were, "Oh, God, all these years I thought that it was *me* that hated my children. Now I know that it was that filthy thing that just came out that has made me have these feelings all these years. It hated my children through me."

When she had relaxed a bit, we commanded the remaining spirits if any, to also name themselves and to come out. The final spirit which named itself and then came out was *sui-*

26

cide. She explained to me afterwards, that she had attempted on three occasions to take her own life. In fact at that time her wrists were still bandaged from her most recent attempt. The Lord did a mighty work within Alice that morning: in addition to confirming for me the validity of *Pigs in the Parlor.* For several years thereafter, before she moved away from our area, I would frequently see Alice at various prayer meetings and Charismatic gatherings in our vicinity.

I realized also through this experience that the Holy Spirit was giving me a confirmation and an underscoring of this *unnatural hatred of children* and its effect upon an individual and upon a family. What we witnessed here was no doubt a cluster of spirits *(hatred of her own children* and *repulsion to the touch of her own children)* invited into Alice by the *spirit of abortion and murder* which caused this perversion of natural affection of a mother for her children: another in the family of spirits related to abortion and murder. However, I didn't fully make the connection until I later heard Dr. Luke's account and the Spirit confirmed this truth for me.

Observations

1. This woman believed the lies which Satan had fed to her: namely that she was a terrible person to have the feelings which she had.

    NOTE: The feelings weren't her own: they were the demon's feelings being *expressed through her.* A situation not unlike Martin Luther's famous statement concerning his attitude toward bad thoughts: "Bad thoughts are like the birds flying over my head. I have no responsibility for the flying birds: my responsibility is to prevent them from building their nests in my hair."

    In essence we are responsible for not letting Satan's thoughts take root in our minds. To refuse to give them any house when they come. They will come, but there is *no guilt* in their flying overhead.

27

2. The demons caused her to think a particular way about herself *(self-condemnation)* to also feel a particular way about her children *(hatred of own children)* and to also have physical feeling *(repulsion to the touch of own children)*. Demons can make us think and feel in unnatural ways. (unnatural thinking and unnatural feelings and unnatural symptoms).

3. Condemnation is usually also present to try to convince the person involved that he/she cannot truly be a Christian if they have the unnatural feelings, desires, or sensations, which Satan sends. "You can't really think you are a Christian if you have thoughts like those, or if you feel that way." His chief desire is for us to give up on our walk with the Lord; to lay down inside and quit: or better yet, to end it all by taking our own life. This was the very classic pattern which he followed with Alice.

4. The next logical step for her, feeling as she did, was suicide. No doubt one spirit had invited another, and another the next, until Satan's master strategy could be accomplished: to remove a pawn from the great chessboard of life, by having the *spirit of suicide* destroy her physical life.

5. The *hatred of children* was truly an *unnatural* feeling toward her children for she told me repeatedly during our conversation, "My children are perfectly lovely children: there is no logical reason whatsoever for me not to love them, as I know that I should."

    The hatred of children is, I suspect, a particularly revealing manifestation of the nature of Satan himself. I am also convinced that much of the child beating and child abuse coming to light in this country today is an offshoot and by-product of the very demonic root which we are discussing here. Ten million abortions in our country means nearly as many women who may have picked up spirits of the *hatred of children*. I foresee more incidents of child abuse coming to light in the future rather than the

28

situation improving for this very reason . . . unless the policies of this country change, and unless the Christians conduct real spiritual warfare against the principalities and powers of Satan.

Indicators (of a need for ministry)

OUTWARDLY OBSERVABLE SYMPTOMS (offering clues to the one ministering)

1. Nervousness

2. Three attempts at suicide

3. Did not have normal relationship with own children

INWARD SYMPTOMS (offering clues to the candidate)

1. Self-condemnation

2. Self-hate

3. Feelings of torment over inability to touch/relate with own children.

   These feelings of hatred for one's own children can intensify into an actual desire to destroy a child as we were to see in the case of Barbara.

Abortion Reflects
Satanic Hatred of Children

CASE NO. 5: BARBARA

"Then Herod . . . slew all the *children* that were in Bethlehem, and in all the coasts thereof . . ." (Matthew 2:16).

"Ye are of your father the devil, and the lusts of your father ye will do. He was a *murderer* from the beginning, and abode not in the truth, because there is no truth in him" (John 8:44).

Barbara's Story

One afternoon I received a phone call from a young woman in obvious distress. She was sobbing her heart out as she said, "I've got to have help. I need deliverance! I have a demon!"

I responded with my standard answer, "What makes you *think* that you've got a demon?"

"I've been hearing a voice inside my head ever since my baby was born several weeks ago saying to me, "Kill the baby! Kill the baby!" She continued tearfully, "I love my baby: I don't want anything to happen to her. I know that's not my own voice. I don't want to kill my baby — that's Satan's voice or the voice of one of his demons trying to get me to kill my baby. I'm afraid. Please help me!" She paused, momentarily out of breath and then went on, "I'm sure I wouldn't really kill my baby, but several times when I've been in the kitchen cooking, the voice has told me, 'Pick up that knife and kill the baby.' Sometimes," she sobbed conscience-stricken, "I've even picked up the knife. I'm so afraid. Please help me!"

She said she knew this couldn't be the voice of God giving her such un-Godly counsel and said she felt it definitely was an evil spirit. When I heard her description, I too concurred, that it definitely was a demonic attack upon her: tormenting her in an attempt to kill her child. Barbara said that she had been resisting it, but had been losing sleep for the six weeks or so since the baby's birth. She had been having difficulty sleeping because of the torment of the voice and the guilt over having such terrible thoughts.

We arranged for Barbara to come at 7:30 that evening to meet with my wife and me at our prayer room as that was the earliest time she could get her husband to babysit for her. I've never seen an unlikelier-looking candidate for deliverance. She was a beautiful girl of about twenty who barely looked old enough to be babysitting, much less a mother herself. She would have looked right at home in the front row of any church's youth choir.

A fantastic transformation took place, however, when we took authority over the *spirit of murder* which had been telling her to kill her child, and commanded it to come out of her, Barbara slid out of her chair and got on all fours and rocked back and forth on her hands and knees, growling and snarling like a mad dog. As she snarled and growled, her face turned very red and distorted into ugly animal-like features and a deep, raspy gruff voice emanating from her kept repeating, "I've got to kill that baby! I've got to kill that baby!"

We instructed Barbara to take authority herself, and to command the *spirit of murder* to leave her in the name of her Lord and Saviour, Jesus Christ, which she did. After a few violent heaves, the evil spirit came out; she then sat up very normally, relaxed and calmly began praising the Lord with great relief. Within the year she and her husband moved into another state, where at last report, they are still involved in an effective ministry.

Observations

1. Fortunately this young woman had received some teaching previously concerning the reality of deliverance and demons and was able to recognize the enemy's wiles and the source of her own problem as demonic. Also fortunately for her, she took action and sought help before it was too late. Unfortunately many who fail to accept the reality of demonic activity, are blinded by their theology and thereby wind up in mental institutions or fall prey to the insistence of the voices.

2. The demon's desire was clearly to kill the baby and it attempted to have the mother fulfill its lust for infant death, even suggesting the method and pointing out the means. (This is the *same spirit of murder* in operation upon the

mother, that functions in others who are directed to murder older victims.)

NOTE: It is important to recognize another truth here — that the presence of the *spirit of murder* doesn't necessarily mean that the one with that spirit has actually murdered anyone. The spirit is there to attempt to cause that person to commit a murder in the future. It may become more deeply entrenched once it has had its lust to murder whetted by success, as in the case of a woman who has had one abortion finding it easier to have the second and still easier to have the third and so on: the opposition of the conscience having been seared. This may also have other more far-reaching effects as we will shortly see.

3. The innocent appearance of this young woman, merely served to better camouflage the spirit which was in hiding. No one would ever have suspected that the young woman had any problem at all, much less one of a demonic nature. Very often until a spirit has literally gained a stranglehold on a personality, there is virtually no clue as to its presence. The only one aware of anything out of the ordinary, is the one affected, until the spirit manifests its nature by taking over in a moment of weakness and causing them to commit an act which they would "never in their right minds" commit.

4. The true, horrible, ugly nature of the spirit began to manifest itself when it was commanded to leave. It realized that its presence was detected and that it had lost the security of being hidden in the darkness of ignorance or fear, and it manifested. Demons often attempt to frighten the person possessing them or the ones attempting to minister deliverance to them. They will try to convince the one seeking deliverance that they are going to be sick, or afflict them with pain or discomfort briefly to attempt to dissuade them from their goal of freedom.

5. Another point we mustn't miss here is that the demon kept at her with a two-pronged attack: First A) the voice

telling her to kill the baby and the second prong B) con-demnation over having such unchristian thoughts. (It begins to sound familiar doesn't it? Satan isn't terribly creative. He tends to function in ruts. Once we learn to recognize the ruts, we are well on our way to outmaneu-vering him and to defeating him.) The evil spirit also tended to wear her down, robbing her of sleep, weaken-ing her resistance until *SHE MADE THE DECISION TO FACE THE FEAR: FACE THE EVIL SPIRIT AND TO BE DELIVERED!*

6. Satan causes us to fear having anyone know that we have evil thoughts. He also causes us to fear deliverance: to somehow fear the loss of dignity. We must ultimately come to the place where we desire our deliverance, our freedom, more than we desire our dignity. This seems often to be a price tag which we must be willing to pay to obtain our freedom — a humbling of self. The same spirit of humbling may also be involved in our being willing to confess our sins. The willingness to acknowledge our inability to solve our own problems, and the humility of coming to Jesus to seek deliverance or healing at His hands is the beginning of freedom.

    "Ye shall know the truth, and the truth shall make you free" (John 8:32).

Indicators (of a need for ministry)

OUTWARDLY OBSERVABLE SYMPTOMS (offering clues to the one ministering)

1. Nervousness

2. Sleeplessness

3. Fatigue

INWARD SYMPTOMS (offering clues to the candidate)

1. Heard voices

2. Torment

3. Feared she would heed the voice's insistence and kill the baby

TEACHING SECTION II

What provision has God made to set people free from this type of bondages which you describe and why?

II. God has provided deliverance

    A. Ministry of deliverance is available

        1. What is deliverance?

        2. What are demons?

        3. What are the goals of demons?

    B. God hates abortion

        1. Satan was a murderer from the beginning

        2. Satan's own hatred of children

MINISTRY OF DELIVERANCE IS AVAILABLE

What Is Deliverance?

There is a valid place for the ministry of deliverance in the Body of Christ today. It has been truthfully stated, "You cannot deliver the flesh"; and by the same token, one cannot crucify a demon! *The flesh must be crucified, and demons must be cast out!*

Deliverance is, of course, the casting out of evil spirits or demons, a subject which seems very foreign to us in our modern, sophisticated society, but it was an area of ministry in which Jesus engaged. In fact, approximately one-fourth of His earthly ministry was devoted to dealing with demonic problems and the casting out of demons. Jesus cast out *spirits of infirmity* (Luke 13:11), of *blindness* (Matthew 12:22) spirits causing *speech problems* (Luke 11:14), causing *torment* (Matthew 15:22), causing *aberrational behavior* (Luke 8:27), and causing *suicidal* behavior (Mark 9:22) to mention but a few. This deliverance ministry wasn't limited to Jesus alone, but rather was something which He commissioned those who followed Him to also make available (Mark 16:17, Matthew 10:8).

We find the followers of Jesus also engaging in this ministry of deliverance as the ministry of the "pattern evangelist" Phillip bears testimony. We can observe his ministry in Samaria (Acts 8:7) where "unclean spirits, crying with loud voice, came out of many that were possessed with them." Paul also ministered deliverance from an occult *spirit of divination* to a young girl who was following after him and Silas (Acts 16:18).

What Are Demons?

Demons are disembodied spirits. They lust to have bodies through which to manifest their own lustful natures. The *demons of rejection*, as an example, cannot be rejected until it is able to inhabit a human body which might feel (experience) rejection. Often spirits work hand in hand with other spirits to accomplish their goals. The *rejection spirit* would often tend to work in conjunction with a *rejection-causing spirit.*[5] The *spirit of rejection* lusts to be rejected, but that lust to be rejected cannot be fulfilled or satisfied until it is rejected. Therefore its cohort spirit must do something to cause the individual within whom it dwells to be rejected.

As an example, let's assume that I am one with a *spirit of rejection.* I might look at you and notice you wearing a blue scarf with a green jacket. The *rejection-causing spirit* might prompt me to say, "Those colors look terrible on you," "You shouldn't wear green with your complexion." Or "You shouldn't have worn blue with that shade of green." Whatever I actually said really wouldn't matter, and even if you didn't dignify my comment with a response, the *spirit of rejection* could still torment me with something like, "Did you see that look in those eyes? She really hates you! Boy, she thinks that you are just as big a jerk as I've been telling you that you are." The effect is that desired by these spirits working in tandem, to produce rejection, hurt, and torment.

What Are the Goals of Demons?

Demons have something more important to do than merely to make one feel bad, although they spend a good deal of time and effort in this category of activity. The primary battle plan assigned to them by their commander-in-chief, Satan, is apparently threefold. Their first and primary goal is to prevent a person from accepting Jesus as Lord and Saviour. Failing to accomplish the primary goal, then the secondary goal is to prevent the believer from serving Jesus at all if possible, or at the least to minimize the person's effectiveness as a believer. They attempt to prevent him, serving up to his potential. Thirdly, if the former goals have been unattainable, the demons attempt to cause the believer to turn away from God; to deny Jesus, to come to a point of serving Satan,

[5]The evil spirit at work here might be one with a specific name such as *tactless, caustic, rude, spiteful, abrasive,* or something similar.

or if possible to destroy him or her. It is certainly unpleasant to think that we have an enemy who is so ruthless, and so dedicated to our destruction, but we do!

We must not be ignorant of the wiles of the enemy![6]

GOD HATES ABORTION

Satan Was a Murderer From the Beginning

Satan from the very beginning has desired to murder every potential son of Adam which might eventually serve and obey the Lord God. From Abel onward Satan's intent has been murder. He has no doubt a jealous rage over those who will ultimately reign in heaven with Jesus, a right which he himself forfeited.

The instrument with which he slew Abel in Genesis 4:8 was Cain. Throughout the Old Testament we have the historical record of Satan's attempt to murder the seed, or to eliminate the lineage through which the promised seed might come. In Jesus' day Satan's plan was still the same. This time he employed as his instrument, Herod, who "slew all the children in Bethlehem and the coasts thereof" whom he thought might be the promised Messiah. Once again we see Satan's hand exposed — *directing men to murder innocent children.* Satan seems to love the murdering of infants and innocents.

Also in the Old Testament we find an even clearer portrait of Satan's desire for the death of infants. We find it expressed in the religions of Baal, Molech and other religions of false gods; religions which required as a part of their worship the sacrificing of infants or children. Shocking as it sounds to us, this human sacrifice still occurs today in the extreme forms of Satan worship in this country.

The sacrificing of infants was and still is an abomination to our God, the God of the Bible; the loving Heavenly Father

---

[6]A complete discussion of demons is beyond our scope here and for those desiring additional information on the subject, we recommend the book *Pigs in the Parlor.* There is also a list of titles dealing with demonology and deliverance provided in the back of that book.

of whom Jesus spoke. He expressly forbids the practice in passages such as the one found in Deuteronomy 18:10a: "There shall not be found among you any one that maketh his son or his daughter to pass through the fire. . . ." (A son or daughter "passing through the fire" was infant sacrifice.) The practice is also forbidden to those who serve God in Deuteronomy 12:31: ". . . for every abomination to the Lord, which he hateth, have they done unto their gods; for even their sons and their daughters they have burnt in the fire to their gods."

"Yea, they sacrificed their sons and their daughters *unto devils*, and shed *innocent blood*, even the blood of their sons and of their daughters, whom they sacrificed *unto the idols* of Canaan: and the land was polluted with blood" (Psalm 106:37, 38). Such practices are also forbidden in the following Scriptures: Leviticus 18:21; Leviticus 20:2-5; II Kings 16:1-3; II Kings 17:31; Ezekiel 23:37-39; and Proverbs 6:16, 17.

In these passages it is clear that the sacrificed lives were dedicated not to our God but to false gods and idols. The God and Father of Jesus Christ would neither have desired nor conceived of such a demonic practice, as is borne out in His own words:

> "Behold, I will bring evil upon this place. . . . Because they have forsaken me, and have estranged this place, and have burned incense in it unto other gods, whom neither they nor their fathers have known . . . and have filled this place with the *blood of innocents;* they have built also the high places of Baal, to burn their sons with fire *for burnt offerings unto Baal*, which *I commanded not, nor spake it, neither came it into my mind*" (Jeremiah 19:3b-5).

Thus it is clear that the practice of sacrificing infants is an abomination unto the true God, and that it is a Satanic perversion of the concept of sacrificing unto God. God is a God of the living, not a God of death, nor does He even desire death.

> "For I have no pleasure in the death of him that dieth, saith the Lord God: wherefore turn yourselves, and live ye" (Ezekiel 18:32).

THE PRACTICE OF INFANT SACRIFICE IS UNTHINK-
ABLE AND AN ABOMINATION TO OUR GOD!

Satan's Own Hatred of Children

Satan has a definite hatred of children — children who are the potential heirs of the Kingdom — children who are the least able to defend themselves against his attacks — children who are the weakest links in the lineage of Adam — children who have the least defense against him and his demonic forces. He will do anything he can to distort and pervert their lives. If he can break up a home through divorce or death and thereby bring upon the children bitterness, rejection, rebellion or if he can cause alienation of affections, trouble in the household, children to be alienated from the parents, parents to be alienated from the children, or if he can destroy any type of normal growth or functioning for the family, he will do it. His ultimate purpose is to destroy life itself. He can partially attain that goal if he can *kill the family unit.*

He is the father of actual murder as well. This is seen in Jesus' description of him, "He was a murderer from the beginning" (John 8:44). Murder is his goal: murder is also his offspring. He is lazy and loves nothing better than to be able to get someone to do his work for him, as in the case of divorce (murder of a marriage) or as is the case when suicide occurs.

He would kill your children if he could, failing to accomplish that he would do the next best thing — cause them to be stunted in their growth as Christians, or stunted mentally, physically or as normal human beings. He would love to have them abnormalized in some way or perverted, unable to function normally as children of God, as in the case of a lesbian or homosexual (Leviticus 20:13).

We often note Satan's attempting to destroy a child while it is still in the womb, if not through causing abortion, then by causing a miscarriage. *Miscarriage* can also be an evil spirit, just as can *sterility* which serves to prevent birth one step earlier.

40

Failing to accomplish his goal of abortion or miscarriage, perhaps because of praying parents, he will often try to take the life of an infant or child after it has been born. We have personally witnessed this latter situation in our own family. Both of our sons' lives were threatened with miscarriage. My wife had to go to bed in the fourth month with each child to prevent premature birth. We subsequently were blessed with two healthy sons by God's grace, and in answer to much prayer.

On my second son's second birthday, he disappeared shortly before a family birthday party in the afternoon. After a frantic search by the worried relatives I received a desperate phone call at my office to come home and join the search for Steve. Just before I reached the house, they found him in a nearby creek — up to his neck in the cold running water with one of the straps of his little coat caught on a branch which was supporting him, with his face just above the water level. God had sovereignly frustrated another attempt on Satan's part to take his life.

Satan hates children. He would do anything he could to kill them. If he can kill a child, he usually accomplishes several things: the child is eliminated as a worker here on earth for the Kingdom of God — his potential is eliminated, wounds and hurts are caused in the hearts and spirits of the members of his immediate family and very often in those of the relatives and good friends of the family. The death of a child is an attempt on the part of Satan to separate us from the love of God. It is also an attempt on his part to give God a black-eye. God's good name and character are often called into question when an infant dies. People ask, "How could a *good* God allow something like this to happen?"

You can almost hear the demons chuckling when such questions are raised. Even though it is unfair and unjust, God usually gets blamed when Satan or one of his henchmen murders an infant; or a child is brutally abused, maimed, raped or somehow warped for life.

Nowhere is Satan's hatred of children more evident than

it is in the case of his attempts to murder children through the hideous forms of abortion which are being employed today. I will not mention the grotesque and hideous means employed to destroy the unwanted occupant of the womb. Any who are curious as to why physicians and staff are often reported to weep during abortions might care to do a little research in this area.

We were delighted to discover that in many cases when we ministered to women and helped them remove the abortion problem from their lives we were also removing a "block" to healing.

PART THREE

Abortion
Has Relationship to Disease

There Is a Close Relationship Between Deliverance and Healing

We who pray for deliverance and healing are not psychiatrists and we are not physicians, nor do we either intend nor pretend to be. We may need to remind ourselves of this truth from time to time, lest we fall into the trap of too highly prizing our experience, intellect and insight to the exclusion of dependence upon the guidance of the Holy Spirit.

We are, however, God's instruments to bring wholeness to the one seeking God's aid, and we should be sensitive to the leading of the Holy Spirit even if it might seem illogical to us at the time.

In James 5:14-16 we read the classic healing passage in Scripture which offers instructions for the sick person as to what to do, as well as instructions for the elders, but there is also a very key passage contained in verse 16, *"Confess your faults one to another, and pray one for another, that ye may be healed."* This passage and others would clearly indicate that at least in some cases, there is a relationship between sickness and sin.

James mentions confession as a step to attaining healing, or to attaining eligibility to be healed. Often we have found that where there is an unconfessed sin . . . it tends to function as a block to healing. We have frequently seen unforgiveness, bitterness, or hatred, as examples, to be very effective blocks to healing. People were literally unable to receive a healing until the sin area was dealt with and then the healing seemed to flow very effortlessly, instantaneously in many cases.

45

Unconfessed sin isn't always the sole block, but so common a block is it, that we normally try to determine from the one seeking healing if there could be areas of unforgiveness, resentment, bitterness, hatred, or other unconfessed sins. (The candidate for prayer usually knows right away if there is, or is not, a need.)

The following case illustrated facets of both of these truths, and gives additional light on the depths of the problem of *abortion's aftermath.*

Abortion May Be a Block to Healing

CASE NO. 6: OLGA

"Confess your faults one to another, and pray one for another, that ye may be healed" (James 5:16).

"Bless the Lord, O my soul, and forget not all his benefits: Who forgiveth all thine iniquities; who healeth all thy diseases" (Psalm 103:2, 3).

Olga's Story

Olga, a young nurse from a southwestern state, came to us seeking healing. She had a medically diagnosed, incurable bone infection which, although not cancerous, was systematically destroying the marrow of the bones in her leg and her pain was excruciating. Olga was unable to place any weight on her left leg and could move about only with the aid of crutches.

She came first to our prayer room for ministry and received prayer for healing. After accepting Jesus as her Lord and Saviour, she said, "I know that the Lord has touched me during the prayer, and the pain is gone from other parts of my body." Tears of joy filled her eyes as she said, "I know, too, that God has begun a healing in me; He has given me a sign by taking away all those other nagging pains and especially the pain which I've had for weeks in my back. But, I have to be honest. Although my leg does feel better, I still cannot put weight on it without it paining me."

I agreed with her that God was apparently doing a work of healing in her body, rather than giving her an instantaneous miracle.[7]

Two days later she attended a public prayer meeting and once again received ministry and prayer for healing. Again, after being prayed for, she told the group gathered around her, "I know that I have been touched by the Lord, for I feel so different. I also felt His touch upon my body, and more of my pain is gone." She said, after hobbling a few steps, "Even though I still can't walk — I know that it is going to be completed."

The following afternoon, just prior to her leaving town to return to her home, Olga dropped by our prayer room once again. She had a request. "I know that God is drawing me closer to Himself, and I want to continue to grow after I get home. I want to be able to find some people with whom I can pray and continue to receive ministry if I need it back there. Can you give me some names in my area?" As we were chatting, a thought suddenly struck me with considerable force and I asked her, "Do you mind if I ask you an 'off-the-wall' question?"

Olga replied with a surprised look, "No, go ahead."

"Have you ever had an abortion?" I asked feeling rather out on a limb.

Olga dropped her head and then raised her eyes to meet mine and with what appeared to me to be a look of relief, said "Yes. I had one nearly six years ago, but no one knows about it but my husband and myself. No one! I wanted to tell you before . . . but I didn't feel free to before."

Her cousin Ruth who had accompanied her to the prayer

---

[7]For a more complete development of this thought and additional teaching on healing see *Alive Again!* by the same author.

room interrupted, "That's probably because I was here with you. You didn't want to say it in front of your old cousin. Right? I'm sorry I should have thought to have left you to talk in private."

"Oh, no, that's all right. I probably wouldn't have felt like talking about it anyway, if the Holy Spirit hadn't revealed it to Bill just now," Olga replied.

I then explained to them the necessity of confessing her abortion to the Lord, not merely as abortion, but also as the sin of murder, and especially in her case as the murder of one's own offspring.

Olga was deeply touched, I think, as much by the sovereign move of the Spirit which we had witnessed in revealing the real nature of her problem, as by the conviction which was manifesting through the tears which began almost as soon as the subject was introduced by the Spirit. She very matter-of-factly agreed and prayed a prayer of confession to the Lord covering both points. I then began praying and commanding the *spirits of abortion* and *murder* and *murder of one's own offspring* to come out. She began crying more profusely and tears coursed down her cheeks and fluid flowed from her nostrils. She underwent a classic deliverance from the standpoint of symptoms, and the fruit of the deliverance was equally discernable afterward in her features which revealed a beautiful peace and serenity. "I feel as though a tremendous weight had been lifted off of me," she said with great relief.

We then prayed for her healing a third time, and not too surprisingly, she was able to walk without any pain at all, and she left the prayer room *CARRYING HER CRUTCHES!*

Observations

1. Abortion (or any other unconfessd sin) can serve as a block to healing (James 5:16).

2. Sometimes supernatural ministry seems to be required such as the word of knowledge (I Corinthians 12:8) which

the Lord granted in this case. Because there has been so much bad teaching, or perhaps more to the point, there has been such an absence of good teaching on this subject from a scriptural viewpoint. Man and man's wisdom have been telling women that they have power over their own bodies, and that they have the right to live as they choose, and if they get pregnant they also have the legal right or option to have an abortion. Thus women have not only not had *good* teaching of the truth, but have, to the contrary, received *un-Godly* counsel (Jude 15) and been encouraged to pursue abortions. Tragically such counsel has even come from misguided clergy. In our own geographical area several of the leading proponents of abortion and the so called "right-to-a-choice" movements are clergymen.

3. She had felt an urging to confess her abortion on an earlier visit but had apparently been blocked from doing so by pride and fear. Nonetheless, please NOTE: *God was nudging her* all the same, even though she (initially) chose not to heed.

4. Significantly when the sin block was removed, instantly, in her particular case, the physical pain aspect of the enemy's work was undone, and the pain was immediately cast out also.

5. There was also an immediate release of her own spirit from a great weight as she herself described it. Many who have been delivered from the *spirit of abortion* and *murder*, have described the sensation experienced afterward as being as if a great weight had been lifted from them. (In all honesty, we must observe that this could simply be the removal of the weight of sin, which others have described at salvation or confession of sin.) Olga was flooded with peace and joy. Her tears that flowed afterward were ones of gratitude and joy.

Indicators

OUTWARDLY OBSERVABLE SYMPTOMS (offering clues to the one ministering)

1. Physical affliction

INWARD SYMPTOMS (offering clues to the candidate)

1. Guilt
2. Fear of being found to have had the abortion

Abortion Begins as an Intent of the Heart

CASE NO. 7: RUTH

"For out of the heart proceed evil thoughts, *murders*, adulteries, fornications, thefts, false witness, blasphemies" (Matthew 15:19).

"The heart is deceitful above all things, and desperately wicked; . . . I the Lord search the heart, I try the reins, even to give to every man according to his ways, and, to the fruit of his doings" (Jeremiah 17:9, 10).

Ruth's Story

Interestingly Ruth, Olga's cousin who had accompanied her to the prayer room each time, had reacted with surprise to the word "abortion" when the Lord revealed Olga's abortion to me.

Ruth said, "I never knew you had an abortion. And I bet that's the reason you couldn't tell him about it the first time we were here. I guess it was because I was here with you."

Later after Olga's deliverance Ruth said softly, "I think I must need the same kind of prayer myself, the way I'm feeling now. Logically I shouldn't because my abortion was for "therapeutic" reasons, but I did have one all the same." She continued after a moment, "I didn't want to have it, but both the doctor and my husband insisted that I might die if I didn't, and finally I gave in. I later learned that my child was already dead. It had apparently died almost a full month before they took it."

"The reason you feel that you need the same type of prayer, I explained to her as the Spirit was teaching me right on the spot, "is that *you too had an abortion* . . . and although the baby was dead, you didn't know that at the time, and so *the decision of your heart* was exactly the same decision made by your cousin. You, too, made the decision to abort, or murder, the occupant of your womb." (I realized that although I was doing the speaking, the wisdom was not my own.) The Lord was preparing to minister to Ruth, as He had to her cousin.

"You are right! The *intent of my heart* was murder also," Ruth agreed.

We prayed for Ruth right then and Satan lost another captive, as King Jesus beautifully ministered to her and set her free from the pain, hurt, and self-incrimination she'd experienced over the years. Ruth also needed to forgive her husband whom she had deeply blamed for years for the loss of her child due to his insistence upon her having the abortion. Her marriage relationship had been adversely affected due to the root of bitterness which had been allowed to spring up (Hebrews 12:15) by letting this resentment toward the husband remain hidden and festering for so many years. Ruth left that day, glowing and was still glowing and bubbling the last time I saw her several weeks ago, months after her deliverance.

Observations

1. The *intent of the heart* here was the key. Whether an abortion had actually occurred or not was really not the

issue. Her intention and decision had been to have an abortion — that was the decision which she had made even though under duress and pressure from her husband and others whom she later had to forgive.

NOTE: The situation here is the same as that of those who have attempted unsuccessfully to have an abortion using inadequate means such as intentionally over-exerting, or intentionally falling, or drinking too much, praying that their babies would die, or having an "unsuccessful" surgical procedure where the baby didn't die, the truth in each case being that the intent of their hearts was the death of their as yet unborn child.

2. The Lord showed Ruth that she had to forgive her husband as well as the doctor for pressuring her to have the abortion. Very often deep hatreds develop in women whose husbands have either insisted or strongly urged that they have an abortion, *regardless of whether or not the advice was heeded.* These hatreds are often about as deep as any that we encounter, and many marriages have floundered or are now on the rocks because of undealt with sins such as abortion, premarital sexual promiscuity or infidelity. *It is essential that we forgive all those who have hurt us or wronged us!*

Indicators

OUTWARDLY OBSERVABLE SYMPTOMS

1. Unsatisfactory marriage relationship

2. Household out of order: children rebellious, not relating properly to parents

INWARD SYMPTOMS

1. Torment and guilt over the abortion, even though it was "therapeutic"

TEACHING SECTION III

How can you say that we must forgive all who've hurt us? If it is possible to do so, how do we go about really forgiving someone?

III. We need to better understand forgiveness

    A. God's threefold forgiveness

        1. God's forgiveness of us

        2. Our forgiveness of others

            a. Three steps to forgiveness

            b. Jesus' own forgiveness teaching

        3. Forgiving ourselves

WE NEED TO BETTER UNDERSTAND FORGIVENESS

Paul has told us that we are not to be ignorant of the wiles, or devices, of the enemy. Many of us have been unaware that we even had an enemy much less aware of the ways in which he can and does attack us. One of those ways is through our allowing unforgiveness and bitterness to remain within us.

Warfare in the natural realm doesn't usually terminate when the last enemy soldier is killed, but rather the battle ends when a particular conflict ends. Conflict ceases when one of several things occur: one, the enemy withdraws from the battlefield or two, when a truce is signed or three, it may end when the enemy gives up on one front. Often this latter condition merely indicates a shift to a different theater of war, as was the case in World War II. When VE Day came, the war really wasn't over yet: the area of combat simply shifted. The war officially ended on VJ Day or the signing of the peace treaty, but even then the same hatreds remained in the hearts of many people for years afterward.

In fact, within very recent years, a Japanese soldier was discovered hiding in the mountains of a remote area, who had never been informed that the war was over. If you or I had been shot by that uninformed soldier, we would be just as dead as if a full scale war were in operation.

The parallel is quite obvious: our sincere belief that there isn't any war is no defense against an enemy who is at war. Inaccurate theology won't protect us from our enemy, Satan. His snipers are aware of the conflict and state of war, even if we have been told that the war ended and that all the enemy's weapons were destroyed at Calvary; and that he no longer exists as an enemy. Our erroneous theology in no way impairs either his activities nor his effectiveness. On the contrary, it enhances it, as it allows him to operate in a virtual cloak of invisibility.

So long as we deny his existence, he can strike us practically at will. If we don't realize that we have an enemy, we are almost totally vulnerable to his attacks. What is even worse, not realizing his existence, when trouble comes, we often assume that we have in some way displeased God and that He is afflicting us for some 'higher purpose.' God unfortunately often seems to get a black-eye in the minds of many people because they attribute to God, the Father, the works that have actually been done by Satan.

There is a specific wile of the enemy that is particularly nasty because it works insidiously from within like a Fifth Column force: It gets *inside us* and we don't even want to admit that it is there, but it is. This enemy is UNFORGIVE-NESS.

GOD'S THREEFOLD FORGIVENESS

The solution to this problem is threefold forgiveness: first, our own forgiveness at the hand of God; second, our forgiveness of others; and third, our forgiveness of ourselves.

1. God's Forgiveness of Us

"I, even I, am he that *blotteth out thy transgressions* for mine own sake, and *will not remember thy sins*" (Isaiah 43:25).

"For I *will forgive their iniquity*, and I *will remember their sin no more*" (Jeremiah 31:34).

"He . . . will have compassion upon us . . . and *wilt cast all their sins into the depths of the sea*" (Micah 7:19).

". . . For thou hast cast all my *sins behind thy back* . . ." (Isaiah 38:17).

God has made a series of mind-staggering promises concerning His forgiveness. In the Old Testament, He made a fantastic promise: He said that as good as the forgiveness which he had offered previously had been, it was going to get even better. He said that when the Messiah (Jesus) came, if we would but confess our sins unto Him . . . that then He

(God the Father) would cast our sins behind His back and into the depths of the sea of forgetfulness. In other words, He said He would see our sins no more. As great as that truth is . . . it gets still better: He also tells us that He will *remember our sins no more!*

These are truly mind-boggling promises. Here we have the word of God Himself that if we would but confess our sins to Jesus, that then He, God, the Father, *would neither see nor remember our sins any longer!* Our minds literally stagger at the implications of these promises: if my sins no longer exist in either the sight, or the mind of God . . . then I would certainly be foolish to worry about them. In fact, if they don't exist in the sight or mind of God, they truly *do not exist at all!* I need never be concerned about them again! I have in truth as Paul says in the New Testament, been "justified." I have become *just-as-if-I'd* never committed the sin in the first place. Once I repent of it, and confess my sin to Jesus, it is just as if it had never happened.

Paul also says, that the blood of Jesus Christ cleanses me from all unrighteousness. This means that if you were to take a blackboard and list upon it all my sins, the blood of Jesus would still cleanse me from all unrighteousness. The effect is greater than if you were to take a wet towel and wash the slate clean: all my sins are eliminated — done away with completely by the Blood of the Cross. The slate is truly clean. It is just as if I'd never sinned in the first place. This in simple terms is what "justification" is all about. Hallelujah!

To apply this principle to our present consideration of abortion: once the sin of abortion is repented of, confessed to Jesus as the sin of abortion and murder . . . then I am clean; and in God's sight it becomes as if it had never happened in the first place. By His own word, He can no longer see nor remember that sin any longer. I am a new creature . . . and it is a whole new ballgame!

In Matthew 18, we see a further expansion of the fantastic forgiveness of God. Jesus told Peter when he was asked, "Must I forgive my brother seven times?" "Not merely seven times, but rather seventy times seven times"; or an infinite number of times. Jesus also said elsewhere that the servant is not above his master. Thus, if He tells us that we must forgive our brothers a limitless number of times, then He too must be *willing to forgive us a limitless number of times.* His forgiveness is truly infinite.

"Though your sins be as scarlet, they shall be as white as snow" (Isaiah 1:18).

Nothing is too difficult for our God! He can and *desires to* forgive all your sins if you will turn to Him.

2. Our Forgiveness of Others

Forgiveness of others is necessary if we are to go on with God. It is essential that we forgive those who have hurt us or wronged us. Anyone who has hurt you badly enough, for example, to make you cry, might be a logical candidate for your list of those to forgive. Whether the person is now living or dead is irrelevant. We must forgive to remain righteous before God, and rightly related to Him.

The scriptural basis for this is found in Jesus' own words:

"And when ye stand praying, *forgive,* if ye have aught against any: that your Father also which is in heaven may forgive you your trespasses" (Mark 11:25).

It is also found in the words of Paul:

"Forbearing one another, and *forgiving* one another, if any man have a quarrel against any: even as Christ forgave you, so also do ye" (Colossians 3:13).

"And be ye kind one to another, tenderhearted, *forgiving* one another, even as God for Christ's sake hath forgiven you" (Ephesians 4:32).

Three Steps to Forgiveness

The Lord has shown us over the years, through many examples, that there are at least three natural steps to accomplish forgiveness. These three natural steps are our responsibility, and precede the fourth step which is a supernatural activity and is therefore God's responsibility. The fourth step is the miracle step which changes hearts and makes situations change and become right. The three natural steps are prerequisites to true forgiveness.

STEP 1. *CONFESS THE UNFORGIVENESS (OR BITTERNESS, OR HATRED) AS SIN* because that is how God views it.

STEP 2. *RENOUNCE THE UNFORGIVENESS (OR BITTERNESS OR HATRED)* — Make the decision to break fully with the unforgiveness. ("Can two walk together unless they be agreed?" Amos 3:3) We must make the decision not to walk in agreement with Satan or any of his works, or any other work of darkness: To sever ourselves from any and all ties with him.

STEP 3. *MAKE THE DECISION WITH YOUR MIND, AND CONFESS IT WITH YOUR MOUTH . . . TO FORGIVE THAT PERSON OR THOSE PERSONS WHO HAVE HURT YOU OR WRONGED YOU* (Forgive them each by name, individually and specifically) *AND ASK THE LORD TO FORGIVE THEM.*

Having done these three natural steps, we can then rightfully expect the Lord to sovereignly do the fourth step — the miraculous part of this ministry and take all the unforgiveness, all the bitterness, all the hatred, pain, resentment, hardness of heart, anger, hurt, rejection and all the poison out of these relationships.

Jesus, Himself, gave the best teaching on forgiveness, and He gave it from the cross. He gave it when He prayed, "Father, forgive them for they know not what they do."

Consider for a moment what He was really doing. We say, "I'll forgive 'so and so' if he changes," or "I'll forgive 'what's his name' if he asks my forgiveness, or if he apologizes." None of these conditions had been met by those whom Jesus chose to forgive that day. He forgave them (1) while they were still in the process of doing the thing for which He was forgiving them; (2) they hadn't changed; (3) they hadn't asked His forgiveness; (4) they were still inflicting pain upon Him; (5) they were still hurting Him, literally to the point of death, and yet, (6) He forgave them and (7) He asked the Father to forgive them also. We can note these seven unique facets of the forgiveness teaching which Jesus, in effect, was giving to us. The seventh point bears especial note: He not only forgave them, Himself, but He also prayed and asked the Father to forgive them!

We can't allow ourselves to be like one little old lady with whom I spent nearly an hour convincing her of the need to forgive someone who had wronged her. (Bitterness was ruining her life; all her family could see it, but she wouldn't admit it.) When I asked her if she hated anyone, she replied, "Of course, I don't *hate* anyone, honey, I am a Christian!" (Christians, of course, *never* hate anyone.)

Finally I asked, "Whom do you like the least?"

Then the bitterness poured forth as if a dam had burst, "My brother!" Then the story of every wrong or slight which he had committed against her over the past twenty years came out in detail. Still, when questioned, she wouldn't admit any hatred. Only with much coaxing did she finally admit to "perhaps slight dislike."

So I suggested, "Well, why don't we forgive him anyway for all these wrongs that he has done you over the years?"

She replied, "Oh, yes, honey. I do forgive him . . .

because 'vengeance is mine saith the Lord' . . . and *He* can get him better than I ever could!"

Needless to say, she wasn't yet ready to really pray for his forgiveness.

3. Forgiving Ourselves

There is a third area of forgiveness. In addition to the forgiveness which we ourselves receive from God, and the forgiving which we must do of others, there is also the matter of forgiving ourselves. Once again rather than giving you my opinion on the subject, let me share with you this truth, just the way the Lord taught it to me.

This truth came the first time the Lord ever gave me a "prophecy." As is so often the case, if God does something in a way that is new or unfamiliar to us, we immediately assume, "that can't be God." That's what I assumed. I was preparing my notes one afternoon for a teaching I was to give that same evening on forgiveness, and I received a prophecy concerning forgiveness.

When the prophecy came into my mind, I immediately thought, "Wow! This must be God . . . because I know that I couldn't have come up with a beautiful thought like that: phrased like that and besides it certainly sounds like something that God would say. So true and so beautifully simple." It was obvious to me that the message was clearly beyond my wisdom. But still it didn't come to me in the way that I had heard prophecies should come. I'd always heard that if someone were supposed to give a message in prophecy, that they would either hear an audible voice, or they would shake all over, or their skin would tingle or that something equally out of the ordinary would occur. Somehow the person would be informed that they were to speak out the word, and it would happen right on the spot, not hours beforehand.

Since none of these phenomena attended my series of thoughts, I concluded that it must not be a "real" prophecy. Still it was *so good*, that I told the Lord prayerfully that since it didn't come to me in the manner I felt it should have, that I would put it in my notes anyway with a box around it; and when I got to that point in my teaching where I felt it should have fit in, I would wait for the "anointing" which I considered necessary to confirm the prophecy's validity for me, and I would give it to the group. If, however, the anointing did not come, then I would conclude that I had misinterpreted His intentions and would pass over it.

That evening I finally reached the point in my notes where the box appeared, and I paused awaiting the anticipated anointing . . . and nothing happened. No unusual feelings at all; so I passed over the "prophecy" and continued my teaching on the subject of forgiveness. When the meeting was over and most of the people had left the room, one young man came up to me and said in low tones, "I really appreciated the things you had to say tonight about God's forgiveness. I needed to hear them. But, my problem isn't so much with God forgiving me, as it is with *me forgiving myself.* I did things while in college that I still haven't been able to tell my wife about to this day, and . . . I cannot forgive myself!"

I interrupted him at that point and said, "Wait a minute, brother, I have missed the Lord tonight, because I had a prophecy for you that I didn't give. It speaks exactly to what you've just said. Let me get it and I'll read it to you."

I then read him the prophecy which went something like this:

"There are those here tonight who have asked Me to forgive their sins. Yet you are still going around bowed under the weight of your sins. — You have asked Me to forgive you of your sins: *I have forgiven you! I have* taken your sins from you. You can stop asking Me. They aren't your sins any more: you have given them to Me: they are mine!. . . . Now, *you* get *your* hands off *My* sins!"

The young man's eyes filled with tears and he said, "Wow! That word was directly for me. That describes my situation perfectly. Thank you!"

The next week I belatedly shared the prophecy with the

entire group. Again several people came up afterward with the same kind of reactions. They came with tears of joy to thank me for sharing the words, as they had spoken directly to their hearts as well. There has been such an anointing upon this prophecy or truth, that every time I have been led to relate this story as I've travelled and taught around the country, the reaction has been almost identical. People invariably come forward to tell me that they really needed to hear those words and that God had touched their hearts and brought relief and release with His message. God so desires to minister to His people and to bless them, that He will even use a "chicken-prophet."

As evil and as malevolent as we had seen Satan's hatred of children to be, we really weren't prepared for the worst yet, which we were to encounter in the following case of Tracey.

PART FOUR

Abortion Must Be Confronted

Unconfessed sin doesn't just go away; it festers! Demons don't just go away either. They torment, sap spiritual energy and await an opportunity or weakness in which to assert themselves.

Unconfessed sin amounts to a potential disaster area. Just as a piece of rotten fruit in a basket of fresh fruit will draw flies and bugs. The flies and bugs don't come because of the good fruit, but once drawn to the site, they aren't particular. They will not limit themselves to rotten fruit: they will spill over and begin boring into the good fruit, and the latter state of the fruit is worse than the former state. How much to be preferred it would have been to remove the rotten piece of fruit from the basket before the remainder was affected and contaminated by its presence.

This rotten fruit example illustrates for us the contagion of sin and demonic activity, as does the following account:

Abortion Unconfronted Is a Time Bomb!

CASE NO. 8: TRACEY

"For the wages of sin is *death;* but the gift of God is eternal life through Jesus Christ our Lord" (Romans 6:23).

". . . Sin, when it is finished, bringeth forth death" (James 1:15b).

Tracey's Story

Without question one of the most tragic cases involving the *spirit of abortion* and related spirits we have ever encountered is that of a woman whom we'll call Tracey, who came to see us several years ago. As my wife and I ministered to her, she finally began to pour forth her story. It seems that she had an affair as a very young woman in her late teens, became pregnant and was counselled by her parents and a clergyman to have an abortion. When she later married a fine young man, she didn't mention the matter of her earlier problems, considering the abortion to be merely a portion of her unhappy past, the memories of which she assumed time had healed.

Having received no teaching prior to her abortion, nor afterward concerning the sin aspect of it, she hadn't really faced the issue. She had simply been counselled that "it would be the best thing for all concerned." Having been so counselled by the "man of God" whom she trusted and who for her and most like her, spoke for heaven, she considered it to be acceptable. (How tragic!) She had however confessed it to the Lord privately as the sin which she sensed deep in her heart that it was.

Long after, Tracey had married and been blessed by God with three beautiful, active children, two boys and a girl. She also became very involved in the work of her church. Nearly twenty years after her abortion, Tracey's past suddenly caught up with her.

One evening after her husband had gone to a meeting at church, she went into the bedrooms of each of her children and proceeded to strangle them one by one. The latent *spirit of murder* which had entered her when she had made the decision to murder her first unborn child, had surfaced and caused her now to *murder her three living children!*

The judge who tried her case assumed that she was criminally insane and sentenced her to joint terms in a prison and a mental institution. She served her time and was paroled.

When released back into society she continued to seek help through psychiatry, but nothing could assuage the guilt and pain. Having virtually exhausted all hope of finding a medical or psychiatric solution, she was finally desperate enough to journey to St. Louis to try deliverance.

Tracey with apparent relief confessed the abortion as sin and as murder, in addition to the actual murders of her three other offspring, and we cast out the *spirits of abortion and murder*. She then experienced, as she put it, "Peace and joy for the first time since I did *it*, years ago!" She then asked, "Could I receive the Baptism in the Holy Spirit?"

We prayed with her and she was lovingly blessed by the Lord as she received the Baptism and began to speak in a new language. I saw her again a few days later and she told me, "I feel normal and at peace for the first time in years and I have been able to sleep through the night since we prayed."

I suspect that Tracey will need much ministry and loving acceptance before she is completely free of all her painful memories and torments. However, the Lord certainly set her well on that path by means of His loving ministry to her.

How truly tragic it is, that THE COURSE OF THIS CASE MIGHT HAVE BEEN SO VERY DIFFERENT IF TRACEY HAD ONLY RECEIVED REAL MINISTRY EARLIER, INSTEAD OF BEING MERELY PATTED ON THE HEAD, AND PLACATED WITH THE IDEA THAT SHE WAS "OKAY," AND NO WORSE THAN ANYONE ELSE.

Observations

1. Unconfessed sin, undealt with demons such as abortion and its related spirits, are like a TIME BOMB just waiting to go off!!!

2. This case underscores the fact that *time alone does not heal!* The fact that the demon isn't currently on the surface manifesting itself, doesn't mean that it has departed.

3. If any one reading this book has had an abortion and hasn't confessed it to the Lord . . . please . . . PLEASE . . . DO SO NOW! Tell Jesus right now that you are sorry for the sin and ask Him to forgive you for it. Then continue seeking through this book, or seek ministry elsewhere. That abortion was not the harmless decision you have been led to believe that it was!

Indicators

OUTWARDLY OBSERVABLE SYMPTOMS

1. NONE . . . except for a troubled and tortured conscience . . . and an inner voice of condemnation.

   NOTE: To differentiate between the voice of your conscience (or that of the Holy Spirit) and the voice of Satan, you must recognize this truth: THE HOLY SPIRIT CONVICTS — BUT NEVER CONDEMNS. (His voice would sound like this: "Yes, you have sinned. Your abortion was sin and was murder, and here is what you must do to get right with God.") HE ALWAYS SHOWS THE WAY OUT OF THE SITUATION, AND HIS VOICE ALWAYS POINTS US BACK INTO RELATIONSHIP WITH JESUS.

   The voice of Satan on the other hand USUALLY CONDEMNS, CAUSES FEAR, AND TENDS TO DIRECT US OUT OF RELATIONSHIP WITH JESUS. His words sound like this: "You have really blown it now. Even God couldn't forgive *you* for *this sin*. This abortion is too great a sin to be forgiven; you are through as a Christian. You might as well forget going to church ever again. Besides, you are too great a hypocrite to be a real Christian. Don't bother seeking help either, because it wouldn't do any good . . . and what would people think of you if they found out?"

2. Unhappiness

3. Murder of children (I'm sure there must have been warning signals somewhere along the line in this case, but I
   cannot document them.) Tragically we have seen several
   cases similar to this one: although Tracey's is the worst.

INWARD SYMPTOMS

1. This woman was in a living hell of torment due to the
   guilt over the first abortion, and subsequently over the
   murders of her other children.

2. Tremendous inward pressure

3. Guilt

4. Torment

We were beginning to think that we'd seen it all, but we
hadn't yet seen how truly contagious abortion could be.

Abortion Can Spread Through a Family

CASE NO. 9: INEZ

"Thou shalt not bow down thyself unto them, nor serve
them: for I the Lord thy God am a jealous God, visiting the
iniquity of the fathers upon the children *unto the third and
fourth generation of them that hate me*" (Deuteronomy
5:9).

"Ye are cursed with a *curse*. . . . And I will rebuke the
devourer for your sakes . . . " (Malachi 3:9-11).

"Thou shalt beget sons and daughters, but thou *shalt not
enjoy them;* for *they shall go into captivity*" (Deuteronomy 28:41).

Inez is a lovely young woman whom I have known for years. We went to the same high school although she was a class ahead of me. She seemed particularly radiant and bubbly this morning, and so I asked her "Why?" She said, "The Lord has been telling me all morning that I should come to see you, and I don't know *why*, but here I am."

I smiled at the confirmation which the Lord was giving, as I had been planning for several days to call her. I had in fact that very morning looked up her phone number and it was written on a pad on my desk, but hadn't yet had an opportunity to phone her. I had been wanting to sit down with Inez and visit with her, in order to interview her and get her permission to write and share the account which follows.

When we entered the privacy of the prayer room, I explained why I was so delighted to see her and what I wanted to discuss. She immediately agreed and began her story.

"You will recall that I have been coming to you on and off for years for ministry, and the Lord has beautifully ministered to me and set me free from a great many things. I was a 'basket-case' when I first came. However, it took years and much preparation on the Lord's part before I was ready to face the issue of my abortion!"

I recalled one of the beautiful but unusual aspects of the ministry which she had received. Inez came on one occasion asking me for help and prayer because she felt she was losing her mind. She said that she couldn't remember anything. She said, "I'd walk from room to room within my house and forget on the way why I'd gone into the room in the first place." She rued, "My own kids say that I am 'spaced-out' and I really am. I feel 'spaced-out' most of the time."

I mentally agreed with her self-diagnosis, as I recalled on many occasions while conversing with her, having her pause mid-sentence, stutter and then lose her train of thought. After a long pregnant pause of embarrassed silence, she would then start off on another topic. It was very disconcerting, although her sweetness and humility in it kept it from being insurmountable. She later told me that she had been an honor student in both high school and college, and I found the thought most implausible before her deliverance.

As we ministered to her, during her deliverance, I had commanded the *spirit of forgetfulness* to leave her, and she experienced a deep deliverance. I tested her afterwards by asking her to name for me all the places where she had travelled or lived since graduating from high school. She spieled off places and dates flawlessly, covering a period of about twenty years and dozens of cities.

I then stopped her and asked, "Do you realize that throughout that entire 'travelogue' that you have just given me, you haven't stuttered or stumbled once, nor lost your train of thought?"

"You're right," Inez exclaimed, tears welling up. "I am free!"

Inez then continued her account, "I came to you a while back when I was preparing to go back east to visit my daughter who was about to have her first baby. I wanted you to help me get prepared to minister to her because I knew that she had had an abortion several years before and even though she wasn't a Christian, I felt that she would need to confess it and get right with the Lord before her delivery. However, as it worked out, He really wanted me to receive ministry and additional understanding for myself.

"By that time I had already begun to hear teaching that abortion was murder and needed to be confessed as such. I felt that there was a tie-in between the *spirit of murder* and the *spirit of abortion*. As we were visiting about my daughter's abortion, you shared more information about the connection between these two spirits and I then confessed to you my own abortion.

"The Lord had done a tremendous job of getting me ready for that day. Shortly after I was saved, He awoke me out of my sleep one night and told me that I was a *murderer*. I didn't understand that for days until He convicted me as I over-

71

heard someone, probably you, speaking about abortion. I then realized what He had meant when He said that *I was a murderer.* He had done a great many things to lead me to a point of recognizing my need of and preparing me for deliverance. One of the things that He did was to bring someone in need to me for help."

(A Case Within a Case:)
Abortion Again Unlocks the Door for Disease

CASE NO. 10: OLIVIA

"The Lord shall make the *pestilence* cleave unto thee . . ." (Deuteronomy 28:21).

Olivia's Story

"A sister-Christian, Olivia, came to have me pray for her. She had the terrible disease Anorexia Nervosa, and wanted me to pray with her for her healing. Before we could pray however, she suddenly looked me straight in the eyes and blurted out a statement that shocked me, 'I know why I have my Anorexia Nervosa, and I know why I have the terrible migraines and period problems!' (She spends four to five days a month too sick to get out of her bed, Inez explained.) Olivia continued, 'It is because I HAD AN ABORTION WHEN I WAS 18!' "

"I couldn't believe that someone was actually saying those words out loud," Inez exclaimed. "I can understand your feelings because I have had one too, and so has my daughter." And then I broke down and wept right along with her. That was the first time in my life that I had ever uttered those words aloud. The words 'my abortion' had never passed my lips before.

"God, as you can see, was really dealing with me. He brought me to full and complete repentance, showed me that I was a murderer and now this! He knew that I had to have something like that happen in order for me to be able to face my *own* sin — to be fully convicted of it, and to get over the initial shock of speaking the words out loud — to overcome my fear and hesitancy, so that I could later confess it to you and be able to be completely honest and open about it."

Inez continued her own narrative, "I had my first boyfriend when I was fourteen and had an abortion the day before my fifteenth birthday. I never really thought much about it, then or later. I didn't really think much about it at all until God got His hands on me, as I just mentioned. I simply told my mother that I had missed my period. She asked me if I'd had intercourse, and I told her that I had. She said, 'Well, we'll take care of that.' The next morning she had me in a doctor's office. He inserted something and my periods began again. I didn't premeditate it, nor did I even know it to be an abortion by name. It really wasn't even my decision. It was of course my sin that brought it about, and I was involved in the abortion, but I didn't recognize it as murder until the Lord showed me that it was. I naturally didn't think of confessing it as murder or abortion at the time, because I really didn't understand it. I have never, until very recently, received any teaching about abortion, so I didn't confess it until recently as being the sin of abortion."

"Have you also confessed it *as murder, in the presence of a witness?*" I asked.

"No, but I certainly know that it is and I will now," she replied eagerly.

After she had confessed the abortion as sin and then also as the sin of murder, I commanded the *spirits of abortion and murder* to leave her body. She trembled, shook, and her face distorted slightly, she coughed several times, and then looking almost like a TV commercial for someone losing a headache, her face relaxed and she seemed to light up.

"I'm free! I'm free! I felt them go!" she exulted. Then she

became aware of another spirit, and said, "There's another one here too. Its name is *Mask*."

She later described the way it affected her as being the facade one wears to appear calm, cool, and pious on the outside, when one is really being tormented on the inside. Pretending, so that no one will suspect that the demons are there. She lost that spirit and also one of *unforgiveness*. The latter focused mainly upon her mother who had arranged the abortion, and on her husband who had failed both to recognize and to help meet her subsequent needs. She also confessed and renounced the sins of fornication and adultery to the Lord and we cast out the corresponding spirits as well. Inez received a real housecleaning!

"It was really unusual," she continued in our interview, "but at almost the exact same time that the Lord was dealing with me about the sin and murder aspects of my own abortion, I noticed that my high school senior daughter was putting on a lot of weight. I asked her if there were any chance that she could be pregnant."

"She said, 'Oh no. Of course not, Mother!' and laughed it off. Since I really didn't know how to pursue the issue, I let it drop even though I strongly suspected that she was. The next month she graduated and went to visit her father from whom I'd been divorced for fifteen years who lived in another city. Although she didn't tell me about it, I later learned from other relatives that while she was there, they too discovered that she was pregnant and took her for an abortion.

She and I have never yet been able to discuss it to this day, but sometime I'm sure the Lord will open her to His truth and we will be able to share with one another. I'm also looking forward to eventually being able to discuss with her my own abortion and the comfort that the Lord has given to me through His ministry, His forgiveness, and His love. I want to be able to offer her that comfort also.

"She later went on to college and got involved in many things that I wish she hadn't, such as hard drinking and the like. She would manifest outbursts of anger whenever I would attempt to mention the Lord, or to share with her about my salvation.

"In thinking back and attempting to analyze my family which has had unbelievably bad troubles and unhappiness, I have come to see several things. I truly believe that there is *a curse* over our whole family: probably a *curse of death*. It may have either been brought upon us by the abortions, which have been rampant, almost like an epidemic or it may have been placed upon us in some other manner.

"I began to see this when I realized that my mother has always justified abortion. Back when I was fourteen she didn't blink an eye when I told her. She just matter-of-factly got me to a doctor. I also remembered that she frequently told me that *I* was an unwanted pregnancy. I have always had the feeling that she probably tried to abort me, or else had had other abortions before I came along.

"Abortion seems to be a family curse," she continued. "I have an older brother and he and I were always very close. He told me that while he was in college, his girlfriend had an abortion. He took her to a place and had it done. Their family history is terrible! None of his family has experienced salvation. His wife had four healthy girls later, but it is so strange: he had three bouts with cancer; one of their daughters has had several abortions, several marriages and is a total wreck emotionally, physically, mentally and has no spiritual life at all.

"I feel as if there is a connection between this curse of death and the abortions. It is as if these sicknesses in the various members of our family are branches on a tree springing out of the root of abortion . . . or else fruit on a tree of abortion.

"I also have a sister who has had at least one abortion. She is married and has a family but her children are all sickly and one is terminally ill. I myself have had two mastectomies. Cancer and death and sin are rampant in our family, more incidents of these than can be explained by mere chance or coincidence. I think Satan has been having a hey-day. I am

75

convinced that there is a curse because of the pattern of abortions and that we have cancer and death hanging over every unit of the family."

I mentally agreed as I recalled the statement in Scripture:

"If men strive, and hurt a woman with child, so that her fruit depart from her. . . . And if any mischief follow, then thou shalt give *life for life*" (Exodus 21: 22, 23).

God is warning here and instructing that even if an accidental occurrence precipitates a premature birth and if trouble (or death) then occurs, it is to be paid for with a life: if an eye is lost in the child then an eye is to be extracted in penalty from the one causing the injury. The same principle holds true if a hand is lost, a tooth, a foot, a burning, a wound, or a stripe. What the child suffers is to be paid for under the law by the one causing the child to suffer.

"Perhaps," Inez continued her thought, "the curse was brought on by my abortion or by my mother's abortion before me. At the very least she arranged my abortion and thereby became legally an 'accessory to the act of murder.' She seems to have been a pivotal key in the beginning of the curse which affects her offspring and their families.

"It is also extremely strange to me that the idea of having an abortion as a solution to the problem of unwanted pregnancies has spread so completely through our family. You would think that one of us might have put the baby up for adoption, or married and kept the child. You would also think from the way my story sounds that we had all planned out our abortions in advance. No one to my knowledge ever discussed the subject in advance of the occurrences. You are the first person that *I've ever told*. In fact, aside from the doctor and my mother, you are the only person except for Olivia who even knows about it now. It definitely isn't as though we had planned or discussed the idea of having an abortion if the situation arose. The subject just never came up!

"Even my husband's family has been under this same kind of curse. His father left his mother when he was born. His father had forced his mother to abort every pregnancy until

76

he came along. At that point she rebelled and refused. She told him that she was going to *have this baby!* This angered the father so much, that he said, 'You have to choose between having the baby and having me.' When she still refused to get rid of the baby, he left her.

"The mother accepted the Lord on her death bed when you prayed with her, but wasn't apparently able to get free from the load of diseases which she was carrying. She was sick all the time that I knew her: plagued with chronic illnesses such as diabetes, heart trouble, strokes, asthma, and arthritis to name the main ones, but there were more. It sounds like she was a hypochondriac, but she really had all these diseases and was being treated for them by the doctors. Her life was miserable and her body was literally being destroyed around her. Unfortunately she wasn't aware of the significance of her abortions, nor was I at that time, so she didn't receive any ministry for the problem.

"Just to round out the family picture in regard to this curse of physical affliction being tied in, the daughter whom I travelled east to be with for her baby's birth had a very rough time delivering her baby — unnaturally rough.

"Also my husband (the present one) is tormented and at times subject to fits of greater depression than his normal joyless state. My own married life has not been happy. I have not found marriage to offer the emotionally sound, spiritual union that I know to be possible. My marriages have both been 'white-knuckle' affairs. I know that I mustn't get a divorce, so I persevere. My two marriages have not at all been a source of joy. I keep hanging on to the hope that the Lord will someday make this marriage what *He* intended that it should be.

"Perhaps the reasons for all this lie in my own sinful past. I feel that in cases such as this where there has been premarital sex (even if only with the eventual mate) and, or abortions, that very often the marriages are not happy ones. Naturally I haven't done a professional study of the issue, but I have noticed among my friends, close acquaintances, and the girls with whom I went to college this has proven to be true. In every case that I can think of, it has held true: the marriages have been unhappy.

"There's one more thing that I feel I must share with you before we close," Inez added.

(Another Case Within a Case)
Abortion's Hold Can Easily Be Broken!

CASE NO. 11: NOLA

"And it shall come to pass, that *whosoever* shall call on the name of the Lord shall be delivered!" (Joel 2:32).

Nola's Story

"Another friend, Nola, came one day to my home to have coffee and as we were sharing she broke down and told me how truly miserable she was. She also blurted out that she too had had an abortion. (I seem to keep running into people lately who have had abortions.) I was able to share with her some of the things that you had shared with me, and especially *that the abortion was viewed by God as murder and had to be confessed to Him as murder.* Believe it or not, *I* then prayed with her and she confessed it all to the Lord, and we broke that curse of abortion and murder and misery over her and her family. She just bawled and bawled and then God gave her a fantastic peace. Isn't that neat?" Inez finally finished breathlessly.

"Amen!" I agreed.

"I praise God that I am now free and also that I am able to share that freedom with others as He opens the door." Inez then said as she reached for her purse and prepared to leave, "I carried the weight and the pain of this thing for forty-four years before I finally faced up to it . . . told you about it, and was set free! Over the years as I came seeking help, I told you about everything else I could think of, sincerely seeking help for the symptoms . . . which I can now see were just the leaves on the tree of abortion."

Inez's Warning

"Inez," I asked as she was just about to leave, if you had the opportunity to send one anonymous message to all your children, for example — a newspaper headline that you knew they would see, what would you like to say to them in light of your own experiences?"

"Hmmm," she thought for a moment and then responded enthusiastically, "I'd just say, I think . . . that abortion is murder! . . . that the results of murder are very grave to the person who commits it. It may take years to bear its bitter fruit — but I and everyone I am aware of who has had an abortion has eventually wound up *paying a terribly high price for it!* Sin doesn't pay — it costs and it costs very dearly!"

Observations

1. Most all of our standard observations might be made here also. Inez's case follows the patterns we have seen developing and illustrates many of them in depth.

2. Inez's abortion was not a premeditated murder as would normally be the case. Her *mother did make the decision* — however, that did not alleviate Inez from culpability. Inez still had to repent and confess her own sin. She was still viewed by God to be a murderer. (This isn't merely my opinion or theory, but rather also what He Himself sovereignly showed to her through her dream and subsequent revelations.)

3. She was a Spirit-Baptised Christian *long* before she became aware of the fact that she was a murderer, and in

need of ministry and deliverance! God convicted her; showed her her sin and brought her to repentance.

4. She received deliverance and healing of conditions *before* the root spirit and sin of abortion were brought to light. Her deliverance from *forgetfulness* and *stuttering* was amazing to me, and the restoration of her memory was instantaneous. She received a miracle of healing when the spirit was cast out (or else it took all of its nature with it when it left.)

5. Interestingly enough the first friend (with Anorexia Nervosa) recognized instinctively that the actual source of her affliction was due to the abortion. Some might try to explain this away as being guilt alone causing her to feel that way, but in any event . . . the issue is clear! She knew that the abortion was sin; that it could open her up to, or allow disease within her body. She very clearly made the association which many have missed. It was revealed to her directly by her conscience or by the Holy Spirit speaking through her conscience.

6. Inez knew that she was a murderer and was eager to confess her abortion as murder; to be free of it and to be obedient to Him whom she loved so much — who had already revealed the murder aspect of her sin to her.

7. The very common *spirit of unforgiveness* was present — directed primarily toward those who had participated in or facilitated the abortion, but also at the insensitivity of her husband, who was incapable of meeting her needs since he himself stood in perhaps even greater need of deliverance ministry than she having been conceived in an environment fraught with abortion and rejection.

8. The fact is clear in Inez's account that this spirit of abortion is a *family spirit*. A family spirit (not familiar) in the sense that it ran through a family: this *abortion spirit* had been manifested in three generations of this family and what was even more surprising to me was that it was in

the husband's lineage as well as in Inez's.

How could this be? Evil spirits within an individual can exercise a supernatural drawing together of people with similar evil spirits. For example, a homosexual doesn't have to do or say anything unusual in a group, yet he will be immediately recognized as a homosexual by another homosexual.

As a further example, a woman who had divorced a husband who had beaten her came to us for prayer over a period of several years after the divorce. At times she was suicidal because it seems every man whom she dated turned out to also be a woman-beater. She would often have black eyes when she came, and so I asked her, "Why do you keep dating the kind of man who would treat you like that?"

Her response was, "I don't go looking for them. It just turns out that every man I decide to date happens to be a 'beater.'"

I believe her: she really didn't intentionally go looking for such deviates, but somehow the spirit within her knew them, and the spirits in operation within them both somehow recognized that she was a "beatable" type. I told her that I felt she had a spirit which caused her to unconsciously select the men who had a *woman-beating spirit*. Her own evil spirit was probably something on the order of a *desire-to-be-beaten spirit*.

It is very possible as we have noticed in regard to other spirits, that two people may be drawn together by certain attractions which they neither recognize nor understand. I'm speaking of spiritual (i.e. evil spiritual) attractions within them.

9. It seems certainly clear that there is an abnormally high incidence of cancer and serious affliction in Inez's family tree. In her account mention is made of more than two dozen cases of specific afflictions in addition to cancer and death; all related she felt somehow to the abortion. In our cases the Christian victims of these diseases seem to

often attribute the source directly or indirectly to the fact of the sin of abortion having been committed. Inez and her friends all felt that the abortions did in some way tend to precipitate the diseases. Now whether the diseases were triggered directly by the abortion, or whether the abortion (sin of murder) opened them up to a specific curse, or placed them in a more vulnerable position where Satan could attack them, is open to some speculation. The latter position seems the most logical to me.

However I am convinced, based upon the evidence that we have seen in these and hundreds of similar cases, that there is a direct relationship between a person being engaged in or having engaged in overt sins, such as the abortions mentioned here, and the person subsequently developing serious diseases. My personal view, as I indicated a moment ago, is that these sins, in some way leave the person open, or perhaps drops their hedge (Job 1:10) and permits Satan to attack. The person is perhaps attackable on the grounds of his unconfessed sin: the unconfessed sin placing them legally in Satan's territory.

Certainly, however, we must observe that all disease is not directly relatable to the commission of specific sins. Jesus, Himself, mentions cases where affliction has no sin basis (John 9:3).

10. Inez observed that the person committing murder by aborting a child pays a terrible price for that act.

11. Here we have a very explicit example of how powerful the truth that we have been presenting in this book really is! Inez, who had herself been a "basket-case" not so very long before, was able to minister very effectively to her friend Nola. Nola was in turn set free from the weight of her sins and led to break the power of Satan being exercised within her own life.

OUTWARDLY OBSERVABLE SYMPTOMS

Inez

1. Fear of losing her mind
2. Terrible absentmindedness
3. Forgetfulness
4. Appeared "spaced-out"
5. Stuttering
6. Joyless marriages
7. Divorce
8. Depression
9. Three bouts with cancer
10. Two mastectomies
11. Adultery
12. Fornication
13. Offspring unhappy: following in same pattern
14. Offspring following in immorality
15. Offspring having abortions

Others in Family

1. Abortions: multiple abortions
2. Adultery
3. Fornication
4. Divorces: and multiple divorces
5. Broken marriages: separation
6. Mental problems

7. Depression

8. Spiritual blocks

9. Hardened hearts

10. Unstable relations with opposite sex

11. Physical afflictions:
    a. Depression
    b. Diabetes
    c. Cancer
    d. Asthma
    e. Arthritis
    f. Mastectomies
    g. Menstrual problems
    h. Migraines
    i. Heart trouble
    j. Strokes
    k. Terminally ill
    l. Periods of great depression (husband)

12. Hatred of children (husband's father)

INWARD SYMPTOMS

1. Fear and guilt

2. Tormented internally

3. Bitterness: unforgiveness

Indicators — Case 10: Olivia

OUTWARDLY OBSERVABLE SYMPTOMS

1. Physical affliction — Anorexia Nervosa

2. Physical affliction — terrible migraines

3. Physical affliction — menstrual complications

INWARD SYMPTOMS

1. Guilt

2. Torment

3. Conscious association of relationship between abortion and physical afflictions

Indicators — Case 11: Nola

OUTWARDLY OBSERVABLE SYMPTOMS

1. No data

INTERNAL SYMPTOMS

1. Guilt

2. Torment

3. Broke down and told Inez she was "miserable"

4. Apparently made the connection between being miserable and having had the abortion

TEACHING SECTION IV

Is it possible for someone who has never had an abortion to have these same types of problems, my husband for instance? Could what you have been discussing explain in some way my friend's problem? She hasn't had an abortion, but her mother did and she herself is being plagued with a fear of dying.

IV. There are various applications of this ministry

A. Not all victims die

B . Others may need this ministry besides women

NOT ALL VICTIMS DIE

In a sense perhaps the infants who are murdered are the "fortunate ones"; as with little children ". . . in heaven their angels do always behold the face of my Father which is in heaven" (Matthew 18:10b). All their problems are now over. The unfortunate ones may well be those left behind in the families which attempted or desired to abort them. A symptom common among such people is to dislike children. While it is true that some people may be born with a strong dislike of children, or with no desire to ever have children of their own; if one suspects that his feelings are unnatural, it could be a spirit related to the spirit of abortion.

Such feelings are not uncommon in cases where the parents either attempted unsuccessfully to abort that person when he or she was still in the womb, or seriously considered doing so. Also although it may be more difficult to grasp, the same feelings may be found in any other offspring of parents who have aborted one or more children. The children subsequently born into this type of family situation often pick up a *spirit of the fear of death* (directly related to the fear of being aborted, or murdered by the parents). This may take the form of a *spirit of fear of abandonment* (the fear of abandonment is really a *fear of being abandoned* or discarded by the parents akin to the fear of death itself). The person fears being killed by starvation, lack of food, clothing or shelter. This fear is one of the strongest roots we have ever found for rejection.

This fear of being killed by the parents is especially difficult for the person to come to grips with, since there seems to be no logical basis for the feelings whatsoever. The parents may have always been extremely loving towards them, yet their own spirit seems to sense that a murderous spirit lurks within the parents. This is a spiritual thing we are dealing with, not a thing rationally discerned.

Rejection naturally enough enters children raised in the type of atmosphere where the parents openly manifest hatred toward their children. It is not as easy to understand for the child or later adult who hasn't seen the hatred actually manifested. Such rejection can be observed in children whose parents haven't allowed such feelings to surface, but the baby's spirit senses the threat of the rejection and hatred directed toward itself from the latent *spirit of murder* in the mother (or parents). This can be present even though the parents have repented of the abortion and really desired to have this child.

Thus, it seems appropriate to add a few thoughts for the one who has been born into a family in which abortions have occured or been seriously contemplated by the parents. It is especially appropriate since it is not uncommon for the offspring of such a family to have certain common problem patterns. These may range from extreme feelings of rejection, to themselves later falling into the trap of attempting to resolve their own problems by means of abortion.

In the former case there may often be the corresponding attempts to get attention at any price, perfectionism, self-justification, self-condemnation or hatred of their own offspring, all seemingly without any understanding as to why. The appropriate corresponding spirits may also be invited in when these emotions are allowed to flourish unchecked.

Needless to say, such feelings or emotional reactions not being understood by the ones experiencing them, will often be used by Satan to try to convince that person that he or she is mentally ill or a terrible sinner. Another problem not uncommon among couples where one partner in the past has been involved in abortion, is that of the *curse of childlessness, miscarriage* or *sterility*. These could also be passed on to their offspring.

I may seem to be going out on a limb to present this theory, but it is quite possible that such couples have brought upon themselves a "righteous curse" from the Lord. Such a curse was brought upon the entire household of Abimelech because of his taking Sarah with the intention of having relations with her (even though she was spared by God speaking to him in a dream). This occurred in Genesis 20:1-18, and the curse of childlessness may be seen in verses 17, 18. Healing did not come until the decision to repent of the behavior which brought about the curse was made, and God's forgiveness sought. NOTE, however, that *it did come!*

To give further scriptural basis for this righteous *childless curse* concept — Jeremiah speaks of "Coniah" who was to be "written childless," a *curse placed by God* upon his lineage because of his sin (Jeremiah 22:30).

Remember, God never leaves His people in a state of hopelessness! If you find yourself in a similar type of situation . . . simply turn your heart to God . . . confess your sins . . . and ask Him to heal you and your condition. (We have frequently seen this type of healing and have numerous pictures on our prayer room walls which have been sent to us of babies who are "miracles" and who "couldn't possibly be conceived.") Note: abortion is not the only sin which can cause sterility; there are others but that is beyond our present scope. (Watch for case histories in a forthcoming book — *Songs of Deliverance.*)

OTHERS MAY NEED THIS MINISTRY BESIDES WOMEN

Another rather surprising truth that we have come to see is that there are others besides the women who actually have the abortions who stand in need of this same type of ministry. Men often seem to be less emotional and less affected by such guilt in the emotional realm, but nonetheless seem to be frequent targets for affliction of a physical nature. They, too, need loving, compassion-motivated ministry.

Less obvious but also possible candidates in this category are those who may have aided the woman in obtaining the abortion: mothers, fathers, sisters, brothers, other relatives, boyfriends as well as husbands. Their aid may have been in the realm of offering encouragement, counsel, concurring in the decision, not opposing the decision, offering financial assistance or perhaps physical assistance such as driving the mother-not-to-be to the place where the abortion was obtained. Their function would have been comparable to that of an "accomplice" in a crime, or of being "an accessory before the fact."

Those in the latter category will have differing degrees of problems varying no doubt in proportion to the degree of their involvement. Typically the symptoms will be essentially the same as those associated with the torment of the woman who actually had the abortion.

For many, the simple act of recognizing their involvement in an area of sin, repenting of the sin and confessing it to the Lord will be sufficient to set them free. If however some in this category find that the symptoms persist, such as sleeplessness, irritability, nagging guilt or feelings of impending doom or trouble, then it would be advisable to go through the steps to deliverance in Section Six of this book, or to seek someone with whom to pray for deliverance.

I began feeling that if the truths which we were seeing and the ministry which we were finding to be so beneficial to women and others in our area were truly universal, then we should begin hearing about them being revealed in other parts of the country also. God did confirm my expectations through other ministers with whom I came in contact, but to my surprise I received one of the greatest confirmations on a Christian TV show, as you'll see in the next case.

PART FIVE

Abortion: A Disassociated But Parallel Testimony

The following account is true and is being included because it contains the same truths which we have been considering, and leads to the same victory. I didn't meet the couple involved until July of 1981, when God brought us together as guests on a Christian TV show in Southern California.

See how many parallel truths you can observe. . . .

Abortion: A Disassociated But Parallel Testimony

Nothing shall remain hid, but everything shall come to the light and in Him there is no darkness (Luke 8:17, I John 1:5).

We come with unveiled faces, for God's glory, for we have renounced secret and shameful ways (II Corinthians 4:2).

Let light shine out of darkness . . . (II Corinthians 4:6).

Now then we are ambassadors for Christ, as though God did beseech you by us" (II Corinthians 5:20).

But thanks be to God, who always leads us in triumphal procession in Christ and through us spreads everywhere the fragrance of the knowledge of Him. For we are to God the aroma of Christ among those who are being saved and those who are perishing. To the one we are the smell of death, and to the other the fragrance of life (II Corinthians 2:14-16).

CASE 12: DAVE & KATHY'S STORY

It is our deepest prayer that as we relate this account of our abortion that it will bring light and will set captives free. For God has said, "Have nothing to do with the fruitless deeds of darkness, but rather *expose* them" (Ephesians 5:11).

After four years of dating, Dave and I became engaged in May of 1969. Dave was beginning his last year of medical school and I had just finished my bachelor's degree in Speech Pathology and begun working that fall. It was during this time that we began making plans for a large wedding in June of 1970. In August of 1969 I became pregnant and did not fully realize what was happening to my body until October. Neither Dave nor I were "in the Lord" at that time and after discussing the pros and cons of having a baby prior to our planned wedding, we decided to "save face" and have an abortion, if possible.

We were thinking only of ourselves at the time and were not aware of the consequences of our decision. All we knew was that Dave *must* finish school, our marriage *must* go off as planned, and that there *was no place* in our lives for a child at that time. The decision to abort seemed to us a logical one, even though abortion was then illegal. We decided, however, not to give up on the idea until every possibility had been explored. There were no thoughts of "were we destroying a life" — the deception was very great. Since Dave was a senior medical student, he began investigating the possible methods by which I could be aborted. The main problem was that not much had been written in regard to drugs, and operative procedures were best performed only by skilled gynecologists. Finding a skilled gynecologist at any price, willing to perform an illegal act, was the real problem.

We were certain we could find some "back-alley" abortionist to do the procedure, but Dave was so concerned about that, he said if it was the only avenue left he would not have me take it. However, for myself, when you're scared — so scared, sometimes you'll do anything. Dave was even considering doing the abortion himself if all else failed. However doing his first abortion on his own fiancee was not what he considered to be the best way to start a medical career.

Together we started the one month quest to find a medical solution to our "problem." Little did we realize that our "solution" was to be the beginning of Satan's work in our lives. All that we were doing was against God's laws and man's laws, yet we persisted. With an invitation like that, Satan apparently couldn't resist.

The first physician we went to see practiced in a run-down area of Detroit. He would not do the abortion but he did give me a shot and some pills to take. He said it would take five days and then my period should start and everything would be back to normal. It only cost us $10.00 and we were thankful the solution was so cheap. Unfortunately it was not the answer and I remained pregnant. At this time I tried a few drugs such as quinine, which Dave got for me, along with some warm baths . . . still no results. We decided after waiting almost two weeks that drugs were not going to be the answer, and that an operative procedure would be necessary.

We then heard that there was a D.O. in a nearby city that was doing abortions and that if we would present ourselves at his clinic the appropriate arrangements could be made. We took the one-and-a-half hour drive from Detroit with much anticipation only to find that he would only do abortions on pregnancies of two months or less, and only for people whom he really knew.

It would not be long now, and I knew I would not be able to hide the obvious fact much longer. It was at this point that I thought we should keep the baby, cancel the wedding plans, and get married quietly. However, Dave reminded me of the quantity of drugs that I had taken and the possibility of a deformed child was something neither of us could face. Further panic set in. Dave was doing a lot of reading and began seeking the instruments he would need in order to do the abortion himself. Neither of us wanted it that way but it looked as if we might have no other choice.

A good friend and classmate of Dave's from medical school told him of a nurse who had an operation by a good doctor in our town. Dave called her and after some persuading, she revealed the name of the gynecologist from whom she had obtained her abortion and how he might be contacted. Dave placed the call that same day and made an appointment for three days later. Our anxiety was growing, since I was now three months into the pregnancy and we knew there would be some hesitancy to do a D&C type of abortion at that stage of gestation. Dave had read about the "salting-out" procedure and was unwilling to take the risk. This appointment seemed like our last hope; and sure enough, Satan would not deny us.

We went to the doctor's office after he had closed, and all his personnel had left. We decided to present the poorest financial circumstances we could and to not tell him that Dave was a medical student for fear he might be unwilling to do the abortion. The physician did seem leary at first, but I think the anxiety on our faces convinced him we were sincere and not a "set-up" sent by the police. He took me into his examining room where a pelvic examination was done to determine the possibility of the abortion. In spite of the fact that I was at least twelve weeks along, he determined that the abortion could be done by a D&C without complications.

Now that the preliminaries were over he got down to the details of when, where, how and how much. The clandestine operation would be performed on a Friday evening at 6:00 giving me the weekend to recover before returning to work on Monday. Only Dave and I were to be there, and we were to have $600.00 in $20.00 bills with us when we arrived. We were surprised that the abortion was so cheap, since sums of a thousand dollars or more were not unheard of and especially if the procedure were to be done by a skilled gynecologist. Feeling fortunate to finally be getting it over with, we arrived at the appropriate time. The doctor took me into his operating room and prepared me verbally for what was to come. I was allowed to keep my dress on during the abortion (afterwards I felt that I wanted to burn that dress). Dave was not allowed to be with me. However, in spite of being told to wait outside the room, he could not sit idly by when he heard my cries of pain. Dave was standing next to me as I went through the final stages of the operation. The anesthetic, a para-cervical block, did not work, so I essentially went through the entire procedure without pain relief.

I wanted it to be over, and for the pain to stop. I kept begging the doctor to stop what he was doing but the procedure was underway and there was no way of stopping until it was finished. Dave watched as our first child lay lifeless in a stainless steel pan at the end of the table; *a perfectly formed child.* As the procedure ended I passed out from the exhaustion and pain of the entire ordeal. Later Dave told me that he held my legs up until I recovered, while the doctor quickly disposed of the evidence. After regaining my senses and one final check to make sure I was not bleeding, he gave us our final instructions as to possible complications and what to do about them. I was given pain medication and antibiotics to prevent infection, and we left the office: unbeknownst to us, but firmly in the hands of Satan.

The next two days were difficult in that I was extremely tired and bleeding heavily. I was still living at home and was very concerned that my parents would find out that this was not just an extraordinarily heavy period. Finally the bleeding slowed and I was able to return to work on Monday morning, feeling tired but much relieved that the matter was over, so far as I was concerned, and that no one had found out.

Two weeks later Dave had to move from his apartment to his parents' home in order to take care of his father who was diagnosed to have metastatic cancer of the colon. It was thought that the tumor was completely removed a year prior, but the sad truth had finally been revealed. The final six months before our wedding were a mixture of joyful and sorrowful moments.

As Dave's father became more ill, Dave spent more time

with him at home and that meant that we spent less time alone together. In spite of the bleakness of the situation the wedding plans were made and all the details worked out. It was our hope that Dave's dad would not only see him graduate from medical school in May, but would also see our wedding in June. Dave was caring for his father at home, giving him anti-cancer drugs, until it was no longer possible to keep him out of the hospital. Four days after being admitted to the hospital he died at the end of April, 1970. The funeral was held on Saturday and we celebrated our wedding shower on the following day. It was difficult to overcome what had just transpired, but little did we realize that the worst was yet to come.

On May 15, 1970, Dave graduated from medical school and one month later on June 12, we were married. The year of Dave's internship that followed was even harder than the year before. This is one of the greatest deceptions employed by Satan: he makes you think that everything is going to be all right when in actuality everything is falling apart around you.

Dave worked 80-90 hours per week and his time at home was mostly spent reading and sleeping. His mother was now alone and this was placing an even greater burden on him and upon the marriage. After only seven months of marriage, the tension between us and the loneliness which I was experiencing were getting to be more than we could stand.

It was during this first year of our marriage that the first vague signs of joint pain began to develop. I was seen and evaluated by one of the internists at the hospital where Dave worked but in spite of the laboratory testing nothing was found. Dave was concerned that lupus might be found, but later put his mind to rest when the lab reports were all normal. God's word says that "what the wicked dreads will overtake him" (Proverbs 10:24). The Lord saw us through those next five months and graciously allowed Dave to be drafted into the Air Force. Praise God, for "what God hath joined together, let no man put asunder," not even Satan.

We were finally able to leave Detroit and for the first time in our marriage be completely away from our families and friends and be together. We finally had time and money on our hands and thought we could really begin to enjoy life. Fortunately when it came time to select doctors to go to Vietnam, Dave was blessed: He was passed over and transferred to Dayton, Ohio. We spent a fairly blissful year during which time we decided to have our second child — only this time for keeps. I became pregnant without much difficulty which made us both very happy after having had the abortion. After eight weeks of gestation, I *spontaneously aborted* my second pregnancy. Fear and disappointment gripped us as the thought came that we might never be able to have any children at all. As we looked back to that first pregnancy, we began to understand a little about the gravity of our actions.

Time passed and I began to have more problems with arthritis of my hands and legs. I also experienced a rash when exposed to the sun in Jamaica. Dave decided to undertake another "work-up" and he consulted with some of his colleagues. Unbeknownst to me Dave was again suspecting lupus, and much to his dismay the tests came back confirming what he dreaded most — Systemic Lupus Erythematosus. He didn't tell me or let on to me that I had the disease and even after consulting a rheumatologist from Ohio State who was visiting the base, my mind was put at ease that I probably just had a viral related type of non-specific arthritis and that everything would be fine.

Systemic Lupus Erythematosus is a systemic disease of the autoimmune or defense systems of the body. For reasons not understood, the body begins to confuse parts of its own cells with cells or material foreign to itself. It begins to manufacture antibodies against parts of its own cells which cause antibody complexes to form. These complexes are formed in all organs of the body and are the basic reason for the eventual failure of those organs. The kidneys are especially vulnerable in that the complexes plug up the microscopic filtering mechanisms which eventually leads to kidney failure. Other organs become similarly affected but to varying lesser degrees. Even the body's ability to fight infection is impaired.

Several months later we left the military and moved to Kalamazoo, Michigan, where Dave began his career as an emergency medicine physician, and I returned to graduate school to begin my Master's Degree in Speech Pathology and Audiology. Undaunted we began to try again for our third pregnancy, but this time it wasn't so easy. Thirteen very anxious months passed before we were finally able to conceive our third child. During that year we went through an extensive infertility work-up and with all things seeming to be normal we continued our efforts. We also decided to try to adopt a child just in case I never did become pregnant again. We were due to receive an adoptive infant just after my pregnancy was finally confirmed. After several more months and a very difficult labor, we were the proud parents of our first son.

My symptoms of lupus subsided during this first complete pregnancy which led Dave to believe that all was well; in spite of the diagnosis of lupus I would probably never develop any serious problems.

We waited approximately nine months and then began trying for our fourth child. I did not really feel as ready for this pregnancy, but Dave wanted to have the children close together since we only planned to have two children. About four months later I conceived our fourth child.

This pregnancy however was to be very different from the previous ones. Prior to and during this pregnancy I began to develop the first of the plantar warts that would eventually cover my face. My arthritis had returned and I felt a greater fatigue than ever before. One routine visit to my obstetrician revealed that I had a greater than normal protein content in my urine. The doctor became concerned since he knew my past laboratory results had confirmed my history of lupus. Dave had told him in a private conversation so that I would not find out. With that in mind we again embarked on a re-evaluation of my problems, but this time it was to determine

100

whether or not my body could tolerate the pregnancy.

It was felt by the doctor that we might have to abort the child in order to keep my kidneys from suffering any further damage. I still was not completely aware of the seriousness of the problem because lupus was never mentioned in my presence and Dave was very skillfully hiding the fact and making things sound reasonable. We waited anxiously as the months passed fearing that at any time we might once again face our one-time friend, but now turned enemy — Mr. Abortion.

Looking back on it now, I am sure the grace of God was with us when we decided that we were going to try to deliver this child in spite of the problems facing us. Thank God for the months that passed and for the kidneys that held up until the child was born. This time the delivery was easier but within days after the delivery my arthritis returned and I had problems with an allergic rash and later the first signs of one of the many skin diseases that were to plague me. Feeling that we had pushed our luck about as far as two people could, we decided not to make any further plans for additional children, but to be happy with our success thus far and the apparent stability of my health. This time of bliss was short-lived however. Six weeks after the birth of my second son I began to develop the full blown picture of acute lupus.

A few concluding remarks are critically important to complete the picture of the role which the abortion played in our lives. When I became medically incurably ill, with an acute exacerbation of lupus in August of 1978, I immediately began praying and began an active search for the Living Christ whom I did not even know for sure was real. I repented of my sins, the abortion being foremost among them.

In our spirits we had know that abortion was wrong, but we kept being confronted with all the tragedies of the battered children in the emergency room — our humanistic thinking was: "Well Lord, maybe if those children had been aborted, then there wouldn't be children dipped in tubs of scalding water or sliced with razor blades." We were against abortion, but yet were unable to take a really strong stand. We needed a revelation from God (particularly for Dave because he was the one who was having to treat and re-treat these children until they eventually died of repeated beatings).

On one occasion when we joined with a group of Christians to pray and fast against abortion (in connection with an organization named Intercessors For America) the revelation came. As we were praying the Holy Spirit came upon Dave and revealed something to his heart. He turned to me and said that we had *murdered* our first child, and that it was through the premarital relations and the ensuing pregnancy and eventual abortion that we gave our lives over to Satan, and we had reaped that wickedness back in the form of lupus. The Lord then said to Dave, "Because you are my people, you are called by my name; because you and Kathy humbled yourselves and prayed and sought my face and turned from your wicked ways, that I have healed your land: [II Chronicles 7:14 — meaning my body was healed abundantly and our marriage was renewed and beautiful.] Also, that there were battered children because life was cheapened from the beginning with abortion being sanctioned here in America."

Then Dave said to me that he was feeling led to share what we had done with the entire gathering of Christians present: people from several area fellowships and related churches. I became very silent and afraid. I looked around at my brothers and sisters in the Lord, and I could feel the pride within me welling up, because I didn't want them to know what we had done. Dave refrained from sharing what the Holy Spirit had revealed to him, but he confronted me when we got home. He said, "Who are you living for: Jesus Christ or Kathy Kovacs?"

In about a twenty-four hour period the Lord dealt heavily with me and broke my pride. I repented and said, "Lord God, if this testimony of what we have done will help one woman turn away from killing her unborn child, then I will disclose this last dark corner in our lives. And, even if it doesn't, I come with an unveiled face to proclaim the truth; to try to live in absolute surrender to you and to your will. Forgive me, Oh God."

During this time of repentance, faced with the task of exposing the abortion to our own personal fellowship and to my parents, the Lord revealed the following additional truth to me: "There are six things that the Lord hates and seven that are detestable. [One of them is] *"hands that shed innocent blood."* Also He said, "do not be deceived: God cannot be mocked, a man reaps what he sows, the one who sows to please his sinful nature, from that nature will reap destruction." He also showed us that through the premarital sex and abortion, we were sowing seeds of death; and at our deliverance which occurred in August of 1978 that the enemy's plan for us was to have me die of S.L.E.; Dave was to die of cancer of the colon, the same disease which killed his dad; and our two sons were to be sexually molested and murdered by two boys in our community. In addition the following Scripture was given to us, "When tempted, no one should say, God is tempting me, For God cannot be tempted by evil, nor does He tempt anyone; but each one is tempted when, by his own evil desire (our selfishness in desiring to get rid of our first child) he is dragged away and enticed. When, after desire has conceived, it gives birth to sin and sin, when it is full-grown, gives birth to death (abortion)."

At the time of our deliverance in 1978, the Lord did not disclose the correlation between the abortion and my illness. Dave being a new Christian of six weeks, baptized in water and in the Spirit, and now delivered from the forces that were holding both him and me, must have been enough as far as God was concerned for the time being. It wasn't until February of 1980, that the abortion reared its ugly head, was exposed, and we were set free to take a stronger stand against abortion for the purposes of God's Kingdom and to help alert others of this deception of Satan.

My most recent deliverance occurred in August of 1980. I was delivered from a *Jezebel Spirit.* The *Jezebel Spirit* is not overt witchcraft, but covert witchcraft. It is subtle, under-handed, unnoticed, independent, unsubmissive and seeks to manipulate and to control those in her home, church, and nation. This spirit when present can be in different degrees of strength in women. For me the *Jezebel Spirit* arose from a spirit of fear and insecurity: hence the drive to keep things under my control. It manifested itself in the form of selfishness. God has shown me that love is not irritable nor resentful, and does not insist on its own way: and that when these feelings and emotions are operating, they are controlling, manipulating and dominating others, particularly the man — the head of the house.

In conclusion, God mercifully delivered me and said, "I had to do it before you and Dave went on the 700 Club, because abortion is the epitome of selfishness and the Jezebel Spirit, and I did not want even the subtlety of it to filter through you for you are cleaner in my sight now than you've ever been and you are to reflect the closest representation of my Spirit as you can, for you are my ambassadors."

P.S. "Pride comes before destruction" (Proverbs 16:18).

We were so concerned about ourselves and "saving face" that the total destruction of our family was inevitable had we not given our lives to the Lord and turned from our wicked ways so He could heal us.

With unutterable praise, glory and honor to our King Jesus — we remain humbly in His service for His Kingdom purposes to be established in us, in others and upon this earth.

With our sincere love and gratitude,
Dr. & Mrs. Dave E. Kovacs

Observations

1. First, it is both important and interesting to note that in this case the situation is basically the same and the ministry, sovereignly instigated by God to set them free, is basically identical with the preceeding cases. Thus, by

including this case we also serve to illustrate the universality of this truth, and remove in essence, any possible bias which might have been introduced by our experiences. God showed this couple, directly and sovereignly, that their sin was that of murder.

2. I praise God for Dave and Kathy's honesty. You will notice that she points out that they initially decided to "save face." Their motive was to avoid the public embarrassment of being "found with child" too soon. Unfortunately many couples are unwilling to be so honest, and attempt to rationalize their decision with a lot of other arguments which merely confuse the issue. Simply stated, this is normally the true reason for the vast majority of abortions.

3. She does mention some of the arguments which the enemy, of course, did bring to mind: the need to finish school; the need for the marriage timing to remain on schedule. She then introduces another reason: "there was no place in their lives for a child at that time." A key motivation in abortion is the emotion (sin) of selfishness.

4. The fact of the illegality of abortion did not prevent their seeking one. Once the decision to abort was made, in the *intent of the heart,* the sin had conceived, and since God's law was disregarded, man's law would hardly stand in the way. This also illustrates the frustration inherent in attempting to legislate morality: hearts and their intents must be changed *before any law can have any real effect.* Laws don't change hearts; only God can change a heart.

5. Satan usually makes it easy when you are seeking sin. He provided an easy gentle step into the abortion path, by the first doctor offering a shot, which was simple and inexpensive, but propelled them upon the route to murder.

6. The proceeding event made it impossible to turn back, or so they reasoned, when she later had second thoughts

about keeping the baby. Because of the initial easy, inexpensive attempt to abort with the shot, it was impossible to back out. (Sin always seems cheap — inexpensive at first, but always proves to be very costly in the end.)

7. The next logic which Satan employed was the fear that the baby would be deformed because of the drugs. Satan hit them with a panic when they would have backed out: fear is one of his chief tools. Keep in mind too that this fear was unfounded: it was a *lie* from the father of lies . . . the baby which Dave saw in the surgical pan was perfectly formed, just as was Dr. Luke's first-born son.

8. Sin-motivated prayer, or in this case a sin-motivated desire of the heart usually will be heard and answered. It cannot be heard by a *righteous God who will hear and answer prayers* that are in accordance with *His will* and *His word* (I John 5:14). God by His own word, and nature cannot answer prayers that are motivated by sin, but there is one who *is listening* to that prayer and giving heed to the sinful desires of that heart . . . and that one is Satan. Satan will work out the details to bring that desire for sin to fruition. Note how he worked out details and circumstances to arrange for Dave to hear about the person who could finally do the abortion.

9. No matter how highly moral the rhetoric would make abortion sound, it still comes down to murder for profit. ($600.00 in this case.)

10. Kathy's desire later to burn her dress, indicates, I believe, an inner knowing or recognition of the severity of the sin, and a desire to destroy and break fully with all connection and reminders of that sin. We have experienced similar leadings of the Lord in cases of occult involvement and witchcraft, wherein the Lord has directed the person seeking to be free to burn not only the books, charms, and tools of their occult practices, but the very clothing which they wore while engaged in occult practices.

106

It occurs to me just now that perhaps there was an element of that same principle here: in the sense that she was engaged in an act of infant sacrifice upon Satan's altar of selfishness, convenience, avoidance of embarrassment. Her involvement was not unlike that of one of the participants in a similar service 3,000 years ago when the sacrifice was dedicated to Baal or Molech.

11. The doctor's promise of anesthetic relief from pain wasn't valid for her anymore than was Satan's promise of an easy solution. Neither the solution, nor the procedure, was painless for her.

12. The curse of miscarriage seems to have been present in Kathy's case also. The loss of a child through miscarriage brought a grim realization to them as it has, unfortunately, to so many others, of the seriousness of their actions.

13. Also present was a "very difficult labor," a not uncommon portion of the curse incurred through abortion.

14. A further curse was recognized by them in the fact that Kathy's body literally began to go crazy as the systems of the body which were supposed to protect it began rather to attack it. This is so like Satan's activity, as to be almost comical if it were not so tragic. He is the author of malfunction and disharmony. Also they recognized the hand of retribution in the other problems which befell them, recognizing somehow the connection with their murder of their first child.

15. How "ironic?" that the doctor treating Kathy in connection with her second full-term pregnancy felt they might have to *abort* the child because of the possibility of physical harm to the mother. Satan certainly had his hooks into this family and was attempting every possible means to prevent them having children.

16. Honesty dictates that we point out an apparent discrepancy between this case and our other examples.

NOTE: It is important to observe that in this case, the Lord Himself showed this couple that the nature of the problem confronting them was primarily one of MURDER. Also crucial to our consideration is the fact that Kathy was apparently delivered only from a *spirit of murder* and was not led to receive ministry for deliverance from the *spirit of abortion.*

How can this be reconciled with what we have observed in the balance of the cases which we have considered? First, let us remember that God is sovereign, and He can do things differently in a particular case if He so chooses without changing the ways things operate normally. (For example, Peter, a normal human being — subject normally to the laws of gravity — didn't sink into the waves at one point in his life. This fact, in a particular instance [i.e. a temporary revocation of a law], did not permanently inviolate the law of gravity.)

Second, truth can set you free. Kathy had recognized the truth concerning her abortion previously and had repented of it previously . . . this fact could very well have been sufficient to set her free from the hold of a *spirit of abortion.* The decision to break with a demon, and to be free of its hold, to look unto Jesus as the only hope for forgiveness and freedom, *can* set us free — even if we don't recognize the thing tormenting us as a demon — without always requiring a specific prayer of deliverance or casting out.

Third, it is admittedly possible that the real spirit involved is that of murder alone, or that abortion *could* only be another name for murder. However, to my way of thinking, it is preferable to cover all the bases, and even if in some cases it might be sufficient to only cast out the *spirit of murder* . . . if there are cases where not also casting out the *spirit of abortion* would leave the door open for the *spirit of murder* to return . . . then I would prefer to *always* also cast out the *spirit of abortion.* (If I should happen to be wrong, then there isn't anything to be cast out and no harm is done, but if I am correct, there is a potential for great harm!)

Thus a matter of practice, I would *always cast out both the SPIRIT OF ABORTION and the SPIRIT OF MURDER.*

17. Praise God for His mercy and goodness . . . when this couple turned to Him. . . . He gave them a revelation of His will . . . and so typical of the voice of God or the voice of the Holy Spirit as mentioned elsewhere, He did not leave them hopeless! He gave them a revelation of His will and His truth . . . and then He led them in a path to deliverance and freedom. Praise His Name!

Indicators

OUTWARDLY OBSERVABLE SYMPTOMS (Physical only)

1. Arthritis

2. Lupus

3. Fatigue

4. Difficulty in labor

5. Miscarriage

INWARD SYMPTOMS

1. Guilt

2. Torment especially after the miscarriage

TEACHING SECTION V

*Perhaps you are right, but how can I know whether Jesus would be willing to help **me**? I'd like to get to know Him better, but I don't have much faith. . . .*

V. Reaching the Source, Jesus

    A. Becoming eligible for help and deliverance

    B. Salvation (a relationship) is offered

    C. Obtaining faith to receive

BECOMING ELIGIBLE FOR HELP AND DELIVERANCE

Foundational to any discussion of deliverance or healing by Jesus Christ for the woman who has been tormented because of her having had an abortion . . . is her having a right to call upon Him by having a relationship with Him. She must be eligible for His healing touch. It would be foolish for someone to consider seeking healing or forgiveness from Jesus Christ if she does not know Him; if she is unwilling to acknowledge Him as Lord; or if she is unwilling to acknowledge the sinfulness of her action. If one refuses to accept Jesus as Lord, or chooses not to accept Him, that person is in essence denying himself the right to receive His ministry, and has no basis for approaching Jesus for anything.

Thus our goal must be to present Jesus' healing and delivering offer to those who have either already accepted Him, or to those who are willing to accept Him, and are willing to present themselves to Him for assistance. Those are also eligible to come, who have not yet accepted Him, but are willing to come into a relationship with Him. (Not merely for what they can get, but who have perhaps been driven to see the extent of their need, by their dire circumstances.)

In order to be healed or delivered by the Lord, we must have faith in Him as the Scripture tells us: we "must believe that He is, and that He is a rewarder of them that diligently seek Him" (Hebrews 11:6). This means that in order to have faith we must believe (1) that He exists — i.e. that He is God and that He is there, listening and caring and (2) that He is able to do the thing that we are desiring to have done. I would further suggest that in order to be able to have faith in Him to answer our prayers we must·also know that (3) *it is His will to heal or deliver us*, and (4) that we are eligible to receive the blessings desired: we must know that we are rightly related to Him.

One fact is certain, we are all going to meet Jesus one of these days face to face, and the sooner we are prepared for that meeting by joining His family, the better off we will be.

We don't have to wait until we die to begin enjoying the benefits of life eternal — it can begin right this moment. The very instant that you accept Jesus' offer of life eternal . . . your eternal life will commence.

The Holy Spirit will begin a work within you right this instant, if you are willing to yield. He will make of you a New Creation! He offers to you a whole new life if you will but accept it!

If you aren't sure whether you are saved, the following will be of help:

SALVATION (A RELATIONSHIP) IS OFFERED . . .

How You May Be Saved

Are you saved? This question may be one for which you have a clear-cut affirmative answer, or it may leave you unsure of where you stand, or to what it really refers. The question is simply asking you . . . Do you know Jesus Christ as your *personal* Lord and Saviour? Have you invited Him into your heart (Revelation 3:20), received forgiveness for all your sins, and been *born again* into life eternal? Do you know, for example, if you had been killed this morning in an auto accident, that right now you would be in the presence of Jesus? If you aren't sure read on.

The question of salvation is an all encompassing one, because when one understands what is being offered, when one is *"saved"* or *"born again,"* it affects every aspect of your being: body, soul and spirit, not just for now but for *all eternity*. There are several things that God wants us to know concerning ourselves, concerning His Nature, His provision and the relationship which He desires us to have with Him.

I. GOD WANTS YOU TO KNOW — THAT A PROBLEM EXISTS . . .

1. *All are sinners and no one can save himself.*

   "For *all* have sinned, and come short of the glory of God" (Romans 3:23).

   "There is *none* righteous: no, not one" (Romans 3:10).

2. *We are all under the sentence of death.*

   "For the wages of sin is *death*" (Romans 6:23).

   "Wherefore, as by one man sin entered into the world, and death by sin: and so *death* passed upon all men, for that all have sinned" (Romans 5:12).

II. GOD WANTS YOU TO KNOW — THAT A SOLUTION EXISTS . . .

3. *Jesus has already provided a means of salvation.*

   "God commendeth his love toward us, in that, while we were yet sinners, Christ died for us" (Romans 5:8).

   "God so loved the world, that he gave his only begotten Son, that whosoever believeth in him should not perish, but have everlasting life. For God sent not his Son into the world to condemn the world; but that the world through him might *be saved*" (John 3:16, 17).

   "For Christ also hath once suffered for sins, the just for the unjust, *that he might bring us to God*" (I Peter 3:18).

III. GOD WANTS YOU TO KNOW — THAT YOU MUST DO SOMETHING . . .

4. *You must repent of your sins. (Repent means to confess them to Him and turn your back upon them.)*

   "If we confess our sins, he is faithful and just to forgive us our sins, and to cleanse us from all unrighteousness" (I John 1:9).

113

IV. GOD WANTS YOU TO KNOW — WHO JESUS IS. . . .

5. *Jesus is God's Son.*

   ". . . I saw the Spirit descending from heaven like a dove, and it abode upon him. . . . And I saw and bare record that this is the Son of God" (John 1:32, 34).

6. *Jesus is God (He is divine: God in the flesh).*

   "For many deceivers are entered into the world, who confess not that Jesus Christ is come in the flesh. This is a deceiver and an antichrist" (II John 7).

V. GOD WANTS YOU TO KNOW — THAT JESUS HAS OFFERED SALVATION AND ALL THAT IT ENTAILS. . . .

7. *You have a decision to make.*

   "He that believeth on the Son hath everlasting life; and he that believeth not the Son shall not see life . . ." (John 3:36).

   "How shall we escape, if we neglect so great salvation? (Hebrews 2:3).

   "Behold, I stand at the door, and knock: if any man hear my voice, and open the door, I will come in to him, and will sup with him, and he with me" (Revelation 3:20).

   "But the gift of God is eternal life through Jesus Christ our Lord" (Romans 6:23b).

   Eternal life can begin for you this very moment if you will make the decision to receive Jesus Christ.

How do we do it?
How do we accept Jesus' offer of salvation?

Paul tells us in Romans 10:9-11, 13:

114

"That if thou *shalt confess* with thy mouth the Lord Jesus, and *shalt believe* in thine heart that God hath raised him from the dead, thou *shalt be saved.* For with the heart man believeth unto righteousness; and with the mouth confession is made unto salvation. For the scripture saith, *whosoever believeth* on him shall not be ashamed. For *whosoever* shall *call* upon the name of the Lord *shall be saved!"*

There it is! *Who-so-ever* shall call upon His name. If you *believe, you* can *now call* upon *His name* and *be saved!* If you'd like to do that now, please pray with me:

"Lord, Jesus Christ, I confess to You now that I am a sinner, and that I cannot save myself — I need You. I cannot cleanse myself from my sins. I confess them to You and I am sorry for them all. I ask You now to forgive me for all my sins and to wash me and cleanse me of them with Your blood which You shed for me.

By a decision of my will, I now open the door of my heart to You and I invite You to come into my heart, to rule in my heart, as my Saviour, as my Lord, as my King, and as my God. I thank You now for coming into my heart and for the assurance of heaven when this life is over. Amen.

OBTAINING FAITH TO RECEIVE

The Bicycle Illustration

Having ascertained by now that we are in a right relationship with Jesus and through Him also with God the Father, we are now in a position to muster more faith than we were a moment ago. Let me illustrate: with an example. If my son and your son both came to you right now and asked you for a bicycle, which of the two would be the more apt to receive the bicycle from you? Your own son would, of course. But why? Both children asked politely for the bicycles. Both need or feel that they need a bicycle; why only your child?

The answer is obvious: you have an obligation to provide for your own child and not for mine. You love your own child and know him. You don't know my son and don't have any obligation to make provision for his needs.

Now let's change our scenario just a bit: let's put you and me in the position of the two sons. Which of us will have more faith as we approach *you* with our request for a bicycle? Will you as your son or me as my son? Again certainly you as your son would have the greater faith: you know that your father loves you, that he has a responsibility for you, that he knows you and you probably also know that he has done things for you in the past. Thus, you as your son would definitely have the greater faith.

Let's now change our illustration a third time. In this instance it is you, not as a child seeking a bicycle of an earthly father, but you seeking from your Heavenly Father that which you now desire to receive from Him.

> ". . . And he shall give thee the *desires of thine heart.*
> Commit thy way unto the Lord, trust also in him; and he
> shall bring it to pass" (Psalm 37:4, 5).

He who loves you with a love greater than your love for your own children, who has known you and loved you from before the foundation of the world, desires to bless you with Himself and to grant the desires of your heart as you come into a fullness of relationship with Him. You now *as a beloved child, as a beloved son,* can approach Him with more faith than you could before as a stranger.

> "But seek ye first the kingdom of God, and his righteous-
> ness and all these things shall be added unto you" (Mat-
> thew 6:33).

TEACHING SECTION VI

All right, I am beginning to believe that you may be right. What must I do? I know that I have sinned and I want help. How can I help myself?

VI. Abortion defeated

    A. Seven simple steps to self-ministry

SEVEN SIMPLE STEPS TO SELF-MINISTRY

(These same steps are applicable to ministry to others.)

Step One in Self-Ministry: Conviction of Sinfulness

I suspect the Lord has already performed this first step for you: that of bringing an awareness or conviction into your heart that abortion is sin and is especially the sin of murder: that you have not merely committed an innocent act, but have sinned and broken one of His commandments.

If the Lord has not already worked such an awareness into your heart, then I feel it will be necessary for you to come to that awareness before any ministry will be effective for you. If a doubt remains as to the things which you have read here, I suggest that you search the Scriptures for yourself, and perhaps reread the pertinent sections of this book until you indeed recognize your action as sin or at the very least become willing to accept the fact that God says it is the sin of murder, and surrender your will to His.

Step Two in Self-Ministry: Facing Your Sin Honestly

This entails facing your sin honestly — not attempting to excuse it or to rationalize it. Determine to be as honest as you possibly can with God, and with yourself (and with your counselor if one is involved). Pray and seek God's help as you proceed.

Step Three in Self-Ministry: Repenting of the Sin

Repent means to be sorry for; to turn from your sin and to dedicate yourself to changing your life; to feel regret, sorrow or contrition. Thus, *you need to be truly sorry for your action in having the abortion, to regret it and to turn from that sin: determining never again to have anything to do with abortion* (other than to oppose it).

Step Four in Self-Ministry: Confessing the Sin

Confess your sin now to the Lord: confess it as abortion and as murder. Ask Him to forgive you for the sin of abortion and the sin of murder . . . and for any other sins you may have committed in connection with the abortion such as fornication, incest, adultery, lying and the like.

NOTE: Tears are not uncommon at this point; even very profuse tears and sobbing. Sometimes a feeling of nausea or symptoms of physical pain or fear may be present, but don't let the enemy (Satan) use any of these techniques to dissuade you from your singleness of purpose in seeking to complete the ministry having once begun it. (He may well tell you that it isn't necessary *for you* or that it is foolishness. He has always been a liar and the father of lies and we know that he doesn't want you to be freed of your guilt or loosed from his hold.)

Step Five in Self-Ministry: Renouncing the Sin

Renounce means to give up; to refuse or resign from; to give up formally any claim to; to disown.

The intent here is to publicly, before the spiritual powers (both Holy and evil) looking on, renounce all involvement with the sin of abortion: to disassociate yourself from it and any other claims Satan may have upon you through it. *Tell Satan right now, out loud, that you are formally breaking all ties with the sin of abortion and that you renounce all connection with that sin, and any others* that come to your mind.

Step Six in Self-Ministry: Forgiving All Others

It would be good at this point, for you to forgive any persons who have hurt you in regard to the abortion, either prior to it or since. The people who may have advised or pressured you to obtain it, or who may have been involved in helping you to procure it: perhaps even the doctors, nurses, practitioners — those who actually performed it are candidates. Another key target for forgiveness would normally be the father of the aborted child — not just for fathering the child, but also for abandoning you, failing to marry you, failing to stand by you, and just for failing to be what you thought him to be. This is not, of course, a complete list, merely suggestions; add those names whom you feel you need to forgive . . . any person toward whom you feel bitterness, hatred, or by whom you have been hurt. Then *confess the unforgiveness as sin. . . . Renounce the sin of unforgiveness . . .* and then . . . *make the decision with your mind: confess it with your mouth, to forgive that person or those persons who have hurt you or wronged you . . .* and . . . *ask the Father to forgive them also.*

Step Seven in Self-Ministry: Praying and Taking Authority

Pray and ask Jesus to set you free from all demons and from all power of the enemy.

Then take the authority which Jesus has given to *you* ("And these signs shall follow *them that believe;* In my name shall they cast out devils" (Mark 16:17). *Take* that *authority now* over the *spirit of abortion* and the *spirit of murder.* Bind them in the Name of Jesus. . . . *Renounce all involvement with them* and . . . then *command them to leave you,* right now, *in Jesus' Name!*

You will also wish to name and cast out any other spirits which you feel may have been in operation in your own particular situation such as *fear, pride, vanity, selfishness, concern over reputation, fornication, adultery, incest, torment, grief, hatred of children, fear of having children, fear of not having children, suicide* and so forth.

I suspect you will find that in most cases these simple steps and acts of humbling, obeying and conforming to Jesus' will and word will suffice to break the enemy's hold completely. However, if after a period of time you find that peace and release do not come, then I would suggest that you seek out an experienced deliverance counsellor in your area and go through the steps outlined above with him. We have found that confessing and renouncing sin and the works of the enemy in Jesus' Name, in the presence of a witness has tremendous power.

TEACHING SECTION VII

Praise God, I'm free! But what do I do now? Where do I go from here?

VII. **Beginning a walk in victory**

    A. **A word of caution**

    B. **A word of compassion for others**

    C. **Your own ministry to others**

A WORD OF CAUTION

We want to be totally honest and do not want anyone to make the mistake of thinking that we are maintaining in this book that abortion is the cause of all sickness, or the sole cause of all mental, emotional or demonic problems; it is not! There are obviously innumerable other possible sources for disease and demonic attacks besides abortion. We have touched upon a few in this book such as UNFORGIVENESS, BITTERNESS, HATRED, RESENTMENT, ADULTERY, FORNICATION, RETALIATION and others. Naturally we have focused upon the problem of abortion, and the problems stemming from it in our consideration of these cases. However it is equally true that there can be similar chains of spirits stemming from other roots such as rebellion, rejection or occult involvement to cite a few examples.

In short, we aren't saying that offering the ministry of deliverance to those who've had abortions is a total "cure-all." However, it is fairly simple ministry, as deliverance goes, and if the woman is truly repentant when seeking help, this ministry should always be successful. In rare cases, there may be other root problems in addition to the abortion and therefore other symptom-producing spirits. For example, today we again ministered to Ruth (see case 7). She suspected she might not have been set completely free from her abortion-related problems because her marriage was still under attack. However, it turned out that this attack was resulting from her having been involved in a series of seances many years before which she had neglected to mention previously. Through attending the seances she and the entire group present had picked up *spirits of divorce.* As we were praying, the Lord reminded her of the long-forgotten seances which she confessed as sin. We prayed to break all ties and she was delivered of several occult spirits, including *reincarnation* and finally a *spirit of divorce.*

She called me later, to tell me that on the way home she had realized that every other woman who had attended the series of seances with the exception of herself *had already been divorced!* Another coincidence? Or perhaps another clue to the insidious poison which Satan secretly slips to us when we allow ourselves to come in contact with him or his agents. The situation is not unlike the comparison in Scripture of sin to leprosy . . . just a touch can make one unclean, and then the contagion spreads . . . leaving a trail of rot in its wake.

A WORD OF COMPASSION FOR OTHERS

When ministering to those who stand in need of the type of ministry explained in this book, remember that it is important to *love and accept them.* Keep in mind that just as you have not, *neither have they, commited the unpardonable sin.* Jesus loves them and in His sight their sin is no more offensive than was yours or mine. We need to manifest His love toward them, remembering that they have probably been hurting very deeply for a long time.

The person[8] who had the abortion was merely doing the bidding of Satan, just as you and I served him in the past before we were set free by Jesus and translated into His Kingdom of Light. This woman has merely been caused to perform a different type of service for him, than we were caused to perform. We need to love and be tolerant of the feelings of others whom we feel to be greater or different types of sinners than we feel we were.

Again, remember they have not commited *the unpardonable sin* . . . and they *are eligible to receive* the love, mercy, and compassion of our loving Lord and Saviour, if they will but turn to Him. Our responsibility is to minister to them in that ministry of reconciliation which has been entrusted to us: the love, mercy, grace, and forgiveness of Jesus Christ; and to bring them back into a family relationship with God, the Father, God the Son and God the Holy Spirit.

[8]There is an acrostic message spelled out in the first letter of the names of the people involved in each of the first eleven cases. Did you catch it? If not glance again at the contents page.

YOUR OWN MINISTRY TO OTHERS

Having been blessed by the Lord with deliverance from bondage yourself and having been freed by Him from the snare of the enemy, you will now no doubt wish to serve Him more fully. There are a number of ways in which you can now effectively serve your Master. Some suggestions follow:

1. READ YOUR BIBLE — Set aside a time each day when you can regularly read the word in order that you may come to more fully know the Author.

2. MINISTER TO THE LORD — You can offer up love to Him as you wait upon Him with prayer, praise, worship, and fasting.

3. SEEK GOD FOR ALL THAT HE HAS FOR YOU — Study and seek to find all that He has made available to you — Salvation — Baptism in the Holy Spirit — Healing — Deliverance — Sanctification — and more. (Also perhaps specific needs such as a healing from childlessness.)

4. SEEK A BODY — Endeavor to find a body of "like-minded" believers with whom you can fellowship and associate yourself . . . "forsaking not assembling yourselves."

5. BE SENSITIVE TO THE LORD — Especially be open to His opening doors for you to share your experiences with others who are hurting and bearing the same burden of guilt and suffering that you have been. This is not of course to assume that this is the only type of sharing or ministry that the Lord may have for you . . . but *please* be open to share the TRUTH with others who need to hear it, as He grants you courage and boldness to do so. Even if you feel you cannot share openly with others, you might want to consider sending or offering this book to those whom you feel might be helped by its message.

"Confess your faults one to another, and pray one for another that ye may be healed" (James 5:16).

"And they overcame him by the blood of the Lamb, and by *the word of their testimony* . . ." (Revelation 12:11).

MAY GOD BLESS YOU AS YOU NOW CONTINUE TO SEEK TO WALK IN OBEDIENCE TO HIM AND TO SERVE HIM.

"Walk in the Light. . . ."

$1.95

Entrusted himself
to God.
Touched by Jesus
and is now

Alive
Again!

The author, healed nearly seven years ago, relates his own story. His own testimony presents a miracle or really a series of miracles—as seen through the eyes of a doubting skeptic, who himself becomes the object of the greatest miracle, because he is Alive Again!

The way this family pursues and finds divine healing as well as a great spiritual blessing provides a story that will at once bless you, refresh you, restore your faith or challenge it! You will not be the same after you have read this true account of the healing gospel of Jesus Christ, and how He is working in the world *today*.

The healing message contained in this book needs to be heard by every cancer patient, every seriously ill person, and by every Christian hungering for the reality of God.

More than a powerful testimony— here is teaching which can introduce you or those whom you love to *healing* and to *a new life* in the Spirit!

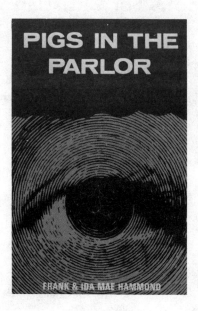

Song Books For Christian Worship

DELUXE GUITAR PRAISE BOOK
An inspiring collection of Psalms and Songs of Praise for Singing with Guitar Accompaniment. Great for Prayer meetings and Worship.
Spiral Binding $1.95

GUITAR HYMNAL
A collection of some of today's most popular Christian songs arranged for guitar or autoharp accompaniment. Perfect for informal get togethers, prayer meetings, sing- ins rallies, etc. Songs include, "They'll Know We are Christians," "He Lives," "Heaven Came Down," "Give Me Oil In My Lamp," "Surely Goodness and Mercy," and many more!
Spiral Binding $1.95

SPIRIT FILLED SONGS
A new collection of songs reflecting The Theme of The Holy Spirit. Songs include "Fill My Cup Lord," "Heaven Came Down," "Come Holy Spirit," and many more. Arranged for piano, solo or accompaniment to singing. Guitar chords included.
Price $1.95

ANY OF THE FOLLOWING ALSO AVAILABLE

[ ] Deluxe Guitar Praise Book $1.95
[ ] Guitar Hymnal $1.95
[ ] "Spirit Filled" Songs $1.95
[ ] "Signs Shall Follow" Songbook $1.95
[ ] "One Way" Songbook $1.95
[ ] Jesus Songs! $1.95
[ ] Sacred Guitarist $2.95
[ ] Sacred Pianist $1.95
[ ] Sacred Organist $1.95
[ ] Guitar Christmas Carols $1.50

. . . ENTIRE SET OF 10 BOOKS, SPECIAL PRICE $16.00

The Liturgical Guitarist

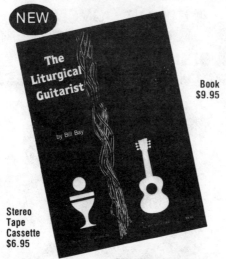

NEW

The Liturgical Guitarist

by Bill Bay

Book $9.95

Stereo
Tape
Cassette
$6.95

SPIRAL BOUND!
360 PAGES! GUITAR
ARRANGEMENTS FOR OVER 320
SONGS! THE MOST THOROUGH
AND EXHAUSTIVE SACRED
GUITAR TEXT EVER COMPILED!

The Liturgical Guitarist is a text which will truly enable guitarists to perform effectively in any conceivable worship situation. The hymns and songs selected span centuries of time, some are old, many are new. Actual guitar accompaniment arrangements are scored on all hymns in notation and tablature. Furthermore, all hymns contain vocal harmony parts. A cassette tape is available on all solos and anthems. It is our sincere belief that this text will widen and expand the worship of God in all settings.

Contains: Music for worship services, music for Holy Communion, hymns and sacred songs, songs of rejoicing and joy, worship, praise, adoration, commitment, service, yielding to God, faith, power, victory, peace, comfort, aspiration, Jesus' passion and resurrection and songs of Christmas. Also guitar solo settings on hymns and sacred songs as well as anthems for voice and guitar.

A BLOOD COVENANT
IS THE MOST
SOLEMN, BINDING AGREEMENT POSSIBLE
BETWEEN TWO PARTIES.

Perhaps one of the least understood, and yet most important and relevant factors necessary for an appreciation of the series of covenants and covenant relationships that our God has chosen to employ in His dealings with man, is the concept of the BLOOD COVENANT!

In this volume which has been "sold out," and "unavailable" for generations, lies truth which has blessed and will continue to bless every pastor, teacher, every serious Christian desiring to "go on with God."

Andrew Murray stated it beautifully years ago, when he said that if we were to but grasp the full knowledge of what God desires to do for us and understood the nature of His promises, it would "make the Covenant the very gate of heaven! May the Holy Spirit give us some vision of its glory."

$5.95

BEST SELLERS FROM
IMPACT BOOKS

137 W. Jefferson, Kirkwood, MO 63122

BOOKS

_____	ALIVE AGAIN	1.95
_____	A LOVE STORY	1.25
_____	DECISION TO DISCIPLESHIP	1.25
_____	GOLD FROM GOLGOTHA	1.50
_____	GREATER IS HE!	1.25
_____	GREATER WORKS SHALL YE DO	2.25
_____	HOW TO HEAR GOD SPEAK	1.50

_____	IS FAITH REQUIRED FOR YOUR MIRACLE	2.25
_____	MINISTERING TO THE LORD	3.50
_____	MIRACLE BUS TO THE SHRINE	1.75
_____	MY PERSONAL PENTECOST	1.25
_____	PIGS IN THE PARLOR	3.95
_____	THE BLOOD COVENANT	5.95
_____	TRIAL BY FIRE	1.95

MUSIC & SONG BOOKS

_____	DELUXE GUITAR PRAISE BOOK	1.95
_____	FAVORITE HYMNS ARR. FOR CLASSICAL GUITAR	2.50
_____	FAVORITE HYMNS ARR. FOR PIANO	2.50
_____	GOSPEL BANJO	2.95
_____	GUITAR CHRISTMAS CAROLS	1.95
_____	GUITAR HYMNAL	1.95
_____	JESUS SONGS!	1.95
_____	GOSPEL GUITAR	2.95
_____	HYMNS FOR DULCIMER	4.95
_____	LITURGICAL GUITARIST	9.95
_____	ONE WAY SONGBOOK	1.95
_____	SACRED GUITARIST	2.95
_____	SACRED ORGANIST	1.95

_____	SACRED PIANIST	1.95
_____	"SIGNS SHALL FOLLOW" SONG-BOOK	1.95
_____	SPIRIT FILLED SONGS	1.95
_____	CHILDREN'S GUITAR HYMNAL	1.95
_____	**HYMNS** FOR AUTOHARP	4.95
_____	HYMNS FOR CLASSIC GUITAR - FOSTER	4.95
_____	MORE HYMNS FOR CLASSIC GUITAR - FOSTER	4.95
_____	SONGS OF CHRISTMAS - FOR AUTOHARP	2.50
_____	LITURGICAL GUITARIST (CASS.)	6.95
_____	FAMILY HYMN BOOK	6.95

Do You Know Anyone With
CANCER?
Here's Living Proof GOD HEALS!

```
┌─────────────────────────────────────┐
│                                      │
│  Name_____     │
│                                      │
│  Address _____     │
│                                      │
│       _____    │
│                                      │
│                                      │
│                                      │
│  For your convenience, you may use either │
│  MasterCard or Visa.                 │
│  MasterCard No. _____    │
│                                      │
│  Visa No. _____    │
└─────────────────────────────────────┘
```

100,000 Copies
In Print —
ARE DEMONS REAL?

FOR ADDITIONAL COPIES WRITE:

137 WEST JEFFERSON
KIRKWOOD, MISSOURI 63122